# Social S

*A Guide to Develop Social Skills for Ages 10-20 to Have Better and Healthy Relationships*

By

Zoe S.

## Disclaimer Notice

This book is written and published independently. Please keep in mind that the material in this publication is solely for educational and entertaining purposes. All efforts have provided authentic, up-to-date, trustworthy, and comprehensive information. There are no express or implied assurances. The purpose of this book's material is to assist readers in having a better understanding of the subject matter. The activities, information, and exercises are provided solely for self-help information. This book is not intended to replace expert psychologists, legal, financial, or other guidance. If you require counseling, please get in touch with a qualified professional.

By reading this text, the reader accepts that the author will not be held liable for any damages, indirectly or directly, experienced due to the use of the information included herein, particularly, but not limited to, omissions, errors, or inaccuracies. As a reader, you are accountable for your decisions, actions, and consequences.

# Table of Content

# Introduction

Social Skills for Teens is a comprehensive, hands-on guide to learn and practice social skills. It presents the fundamental principles of social interaction in simple, straightforward course.

I have written this book to serve as the advice I so crucially needed amid my own social challenges. As a child, I was the most socially awkward child you could wish to meet.

This guide is for the teens who want to become social and establish good social connections. It is a compilation of the social principles I have learned over the course of a lifetime of personal social skills study, as well as the techniques I developed while providing hundreds of hours of social skills coaching. It gives precise blueprints for fundamental skills like speech and body language for teens to learn and practice. It also provides concise explanations for complicated issues such as empathy and making friends.

Few would argue against the concept that the group of people you associate with has a greater influence on the path of your life than any other thing. This is true not only for extroverts but also for introverts. Regardless of how much time we choose to spend with others, the connections we make have a profound effect on our lives.

Consider your most cherished recollections. How many were conducted without the involvement of others? There are probably few or none. How about the times in your life when you experienced the biggest personal growth? Were you not guided or supported by friends or mentors? Even the most trying circumstances in your life are virtually always improved by others.

This book is centered on a basic premise: the importance of people and friendships in our lives. They are significant enough to justify exerting effort to improve our friendships and family relationships.

The people with whom you engage can be classified into three types. They are acquaintances, friends, and intimate friends. Each of these categories needs you to share a unique aspect of yourself and contributes significantly to your life.

After reading this book, you should be able to convert strangers into friends. You will master the art of conversation and how to reveal the greatest parts of yourself authentically and honestly. You will discover how to create new friends and be the type of friend that others desire. Finally, you will discover how to cultivate a network of friends with whom you may share encouragement, quality time, and affection.

If you are not sure why you do not have more friends or if the process of making friends bothers you as a teen, you can start again and create an entirely new social life. This book should clear the air if you have strong social skills but are perplexed by some social circumstances. Even if you already have wonderful friends and have no difficulty making new ones, I hope you will pick up a few tips to improve your connections. Some connections last a lifetime and even a minor improvement can be significant.

Few people excel at any talent without deliberate thinking and practice, and social skills are no exception. I transformed from an introvert who was too nervous about interacting with friends of friends to someone who has amazing friends all over the world and a core group of close friends with whom I share a great deal of my life. By understanding the skills and ideas behind social interaction, whether with strangers or best friends, you can break free from any mold and develop superhuman social skills.

This book is a detailed guide to social reintegration for teens who struggle in establishing social connections. While there are titles that focus exclusively on shyness or conversation skills, this one covers all you need to know in one spot. When I was younger, I grappled with all of these challenges and created this as the advice I wished would have received at the time.

This book teaches the foundations that you may have missed while growing up. It addresses impediments that arise only for individuals who have struggled socially for the majority of their lives.

# Chapter 1: The Foundations

If you were terrible at something, say badminton, you would probably want to improve. You would not be self-conscious, but you would take steps to improve. Perhaps you would study books, watch videos, enlist the assistance of friends, or enroll in lessons. Whichever path you choose; you would have to practice. You would evaluate your progress and the outcomes of your practice and make any course modifications.

When you ultimately become proficient at badminton, you might offer a story of how you improved and anticipate that others would view your course of action favorably. You identified an area of your life that needed improvement, devised a plan to transform it into a strength, carried out your plan, and succeeded.

Even though we use the term "social skill," we view it as inborn mystic energy rather than an attainable ability. We behave as if social skills, like hair color or eye color, are genetically predetermined. If we lack social skills or our social skills are inconsistent, we often believe that this is what we got by destiny.

Perhaps this stems from the belief that while mastering badminton does not alter one's personality, developing social skills can. Our interactions with people are so central to our life experiences that we connect them with who we are. And there is some validity to that as well. How we present ourselves to others shapes their perception of who we are. The same individual is regarded as an idiot and a saint by two distinct groups of people, not because he is either, but because of how he treats them.

Change, in general, is frightening, especially for those who know the person who is changing. Insecurities and doubts about motives surface. Why is he attempting to transform into someone he is not? Why is he unable to be himself?

However, what is self-improvement if it does not result in us being better versions of ourselves? We preserve the positive aspects of ourselves, perhaps even improve them, but we also attack and lessen or eradicate our shortcomings. We all have shortcomings and can improve.

It is time to recognize social skills as skills and remove any stigma associated with their development. We should applaud individuals who take the courageous step of admitting that something so fundamental to their existence needs improvement, even if that individual is ourselves. Yes, we would change as individuals, but that was always going to happen. We change constantly, and most of the time in tiny amounts, so why not direct that change into something bigger and more influential?

## 1.1 How to Use this Book?

You may use the guide in any way you like. Read the entire thing in one sitting. Navigate to the sections that most interest you. Read it aloud to your cat. The world is indeed your oyster.

However, if you want to get the most out of the book, I have some recommendations for you.

**Continue reading the guide in order**

The subsequent chapters refer to earlier concepts and discuss more sophisticated subjects. It is especially critical to read in order inside chapters, as the components of each chapter build directly on one another. You are welcome to hop around as much as you wish, but if a particular chapter or section does not make sense, the best course of action is to go back and read what you missed.

**Apply what you have learned**

The only way to understand how to apply the principles in the guide to the actual world is to get out there and do so. Therefore, set aside some time each day for practice. Watch television with the volume turned down and observe the performers' body language until you distinguish between comfort and discomfort. Engage in conversation with a coworker and practice keeping the conversational flow. Spend some time at the end of the day thinking about your social skills goals. Choose a social skill you wish to improve and devote some time each day to practicing it.

**Slowly but steadily, study**

While it is feasible to read the full guide in one sitting, there is much information to absorb. Allow yourself to absorb whatever you can truly. I propose reading a little each day, perhaps a subsection of a chapter or two, and then practicing what you have read throughout the day.

**Don't go it alone!**

Solicit assistance from friends, family, and mentors on your social skills journey. Your support network can be an invaluable source of guidance and encouragement. It would help if you approached the guide with certain objectives in mind. While improving your social skills for the sake of improving your social skills is admirable, it is difficult to stay motivated without specific goals. Having specific goals enables you to monitor your progress and stay motivated.

**Supplement the guide with additional sources**

While this book has a wealth of valuable information, more social skills resources can supplement what you learn in this book.

Regardless of how you choose to use the guide, remember that practice and tenacity are the two most important components of success. Be rigorous in practicing the skills you acquire. If you do, you will be well on your path to social success.

# 1.2 Set Goals for Your Social Skills Journey

My close friend frequently inquires, "Where are you, and where are you going?"

He asks this because he feels that life is a journey. The person you were yesterday was not the person you would be tomorrow because today's experiences did not form the person you were yesterday. You will evolve throughout your life.

It is unavoidable.

However, how you transform is entirely up to you.

You will change regardless of whether you spend your weekend watching television or assisting a family in building a home, but it is entirely up to you whether you pick up the remote or the hammer. Regrettably, it is difficult to make a positive change. It is all too easy to put off making a positive change until later or to give up as soon as the process becomes inconvenient.

That is why it is critical to know where you are and where you are heading. When you do not, it is like embarking on a lengthy adventure without a map. You will have no notion where to begin, and you will have no way of knowing if you are progressing toward your goal or simply meandering in circles.

However, if you understand where you are and where you want to go, you can make a map.

You can plan your journey and mentally prepare for any challenges that may arise along the road. While the journey may still be lengthy, you know you will not give up since you focus on your target.

Knowing where you are in terms of social skills implies that you are aware of your current social strengths and limits and the impact those strengths and limitations have on your life. And knowing where you are heading implies that you have a precise set of social goals in mind, as well as a strategy for achieving those goals.

I have included some questions to assist you in determining where you are and where you are heading, and I encourage you to consider them thoroughly. Allow the questions to guide your thinking, and do not get too caught up in how you react to each one. There are no correct or incorrect answers; the questions serve solely to guide your thinking.

Where are you? What are your social strengths? Social strengths are the excellent characteristics that you bring to partnerships and social interactions. They can be social skills, but they do not have to be. Loyalty to friends and a genuine desire to learn about others qualify as social characteristics, even if they are not necessarily social skills.

Consider the most rewarding relationships in your life. These could be present connections or ones from your past. How were those relationships? What makes such partnerships so special? How did those partnerships impact your life? How have you attempted to improve your social skills in the past? Have those strategies been effective? If so, what factors contributed to their success? If not, what would assist you in becoming more effective this time around?

What are the present gaps in your knowledge of social skills? What aspects of social contact do you struggle with or do not understand? Why did you decide to begin reading? How can you improve your social skills?

Where are you going? What are the practical areas of social skills that you wish to improve? The "nuts and bolts" of social interaction are practical skills. They include things like facilitating easy interactions, comprehending how others feel, and avoiding unnecessary conflict. What are your "short term" social skills goals? Several instances include making a new friend, having a good time at a social event, or expanding your relationship with an existing friend. These are the objectives that you believe can be fulfilled within the next several weeks or months.

What are your long-term social skills goals? Several examples include having someone you consider a close friend or feeling entirely at ease in social circumstances. Who are the people who can assist you on your social skills journey? These could be friends, family members, or mentors who can support you, function as a sounding board, or give a safe space for you to practice your social skills. What motivates you to embark on this path of social skill development? How can you assist yourself in remaining motivated, even when the path becomes difficult?

I invite you to jot down your responses to these questions and return to them as you progress through the book.

As your comprehension of social skills increases, your understanding of where you are and where you are headed will become more accurate. Take the time to ask yourself, "Where am I at this moment and where am I going?" and you will ensure that you continue to grow on the proper path.

Additionally, keep in mind that slow growth is still growth. It may take a long time to attain your goals or even to notice any progress at all. However, do not surrender. Each time you try something new or acquire a new skill, you make progress. Learning social skills is a marathon, not a sprint. It does not matter how quickly you achieve your goals; what matters is that you continue on your journey.

## 1.3 Social Skills and Manipulation

I once delivered a speech at a university, followed by a Q&A session. The students' questions were incisive, resulting in an engaging conversation. Near the end, a professor questioned, very accusatorily, whether practicing social skills wasn't simply manipulating and lying to people.

Many people believe that enhancing one's social skills purposefully is manipulative, fraudulent, or dishonest. If you are anything like that professor, nothing I say will likely sway your decision. As far as I can tell, this reaction is motivated by a sense of uneasiness that cannot be eradicated with a few pages of explanation.

Learning social skills, in my opinion, is the polar opposite. To me, it is the practice of becoming the best possible person and maximizing what you have to offer others. It is about communicating your identity as plainly as possible and removing impediments to understanding others with the same clarity. It is about truly comprehending what others seek in a conversation or a buddy and attempting to provide them with that same thing if you are capable. We constantly engage in behaviors to generate a response from another person. That is not manipulation in and of itself. I may tell a joke to amuse a friend. Technically, I have acted to elicit a response from him, but few would describe that as manipulating.

Manipulation implies hidden objectives. It means that we can convince someone to act contrary to their will or best interests by coaxing them or projecting a false image of ourselves.

That is not the purpose of social skills development. The goal is to gain a deeper understanding of what other people truly desire, find where that desire overlaps with your own, and acquire the social tools necessary to provide both parties with what they desire.

It is also about recognizing when there is not an intersection and proceeding accordingly. Self-awareness, situational awareness,

effective communication skills, and an appreciation for humor, empathy, and social dynamics are the tools we employ to do this.

Perhaps the easiest litmus test to comprehend emotionally is this: if a stranger worked hard to improve his conversational skills, would you hold it against him if you had a terrific conversation with him? If you discovered that one of your closest friends worked tirelessly to be the best friend they could be, would you be upset or flattered?

I will be unapologetically analytical in this book, analyzing and quantifying areas of social skills rarely discussed. We will discuss power dynamics, our worth as friends, opportunity costs, and time management. Whether or not we recognize these and other elements, they undergird our social interactions and significantly impact the quality of our relationships. While some find these subjects distasteful, if not offensive, it is difficult to make a better sausage if you don't look inside the factory.

# 1.4 The Goals of This Book

Our society is experiencing a social crisis. Our social engagement is being tapped away from the physical world and into cyberspace. We may well have dozens of friends on social media with whom we keep up with their every move but never have a real discussion. Because so much of our communication is electronic, we have dulled some of the only valuable

characteristics in person: timing, listening, yielding, and understanding body language and facial expressions.

Perhaps you are experiencing the consequences of this degeneration. You have many friends, but few, if any, on whom you can truly rely, and even fewer who truly understand you. When you spend time with your friends, the experience is not quite as pleasurable as you recall from your youth.

On an individual basis, the solution to this challenge is to develop certain social skills to a basic level. Before we get into the specifics of developing these social skills, I'd want to outline the objectives we'll be pursuing and why they are critical.

**Be at Ease with All Social Levels.**

A socially skilled individual can interact with members of all social strata. Not necessarily all people, but all types of people. This is a valuable talent and a critical benchmark. You may rely on shared characteristics with a clone of yourself, but you must genuinely exercise your social skills while attempting to connect with someone you share little. If you cannot do so, you may be adept at relating to people with whom you are compatible but lack social skills.

The commonality is a shortcut to rapport and one that should be used whenever possible. However, the most engaging talks and friendships can occur between people who have little in common. After all, having fewer things in common implies that there is more uncharted terrain to explore.

Developing this ability takes venturing outside one's comfort zone and confronting buried uneasiness. On the one hand, it is possible to feel inferior to individuals you like, as if you have nothing to contribute to the connection. A lack of commonality can be difficult to overcome on both sides, especially if your backgrounds are different and the other person feels intimidated by it.

Someone at ease in interacting with and befriending people from various strata of society would be at ease in almost any setting, confident in his ability to contribute to every engagement in which he participates. He will have more possibilities to share his knowledge with others and the opportunity to learn from situations he may never have firsthand.

**Be A Net Contributor**

Apart from simply getting along with individuals from all sectors of society, you want to be a net positive force in each social scenario you find yourself in. If you join someone who is eating alone, it should improve their lunch. If a group of friends is drinking tea and you are invited, your presence should enhance the experience for everyone. And attend a large party or event, even though your effect is proportionately reduced due to the event's size. Individuals with whom you connect should be grateful that you attended.

Being a net contributor is distinct from simply not being a net loser. Being merely neutral is frequently detrimental, as you are occupying an attendance spot that another potential addition might have filled. It is critical to contribute to social settings actively.

The majority of social circles are composed of concentric circles. There is a small inner nucleus of individuals who organize and are invited to everything without whom events would not occur. Then there is the next ring of people who are always welcome but never attempt to replace a nucleus member. Outside of those two rings are individuals who are typically invited, but only if space allows. Or perhaps they have personality traits that make them incompatible with other circle members, necessitating that the core group decides who is invited and who is not.

The nucleus is made up of individuals who are net contributors and who organize events. The following circle includes those who are also net contributors. Further out in the circle are those who are "not negative." They occasionally contribute and occasionally serve as a neutral. They're good to have around but not certain enough to attend every occasion. Beyond those rings are individuals who are either net negatives at times or always.

By ensuring that you are always a net addition, even if little, you will significantly improve the number of events to which you are invited. Apart from being enjoyable and beneficial, these invites will allow you to practice your social skills, generating a virtuous cycle.

**Create a high-quality friend group.**

Except for your everyday behaviors, nothing will have as much influence on your life as your core friend group. Whether you are conscious of it or not, individuals closest to you are continuously molding and influencing you. You will get guidance from them, pick up on their mannerisms and habits, and perhaps even subconsciously embrace some of their viewpoints.

The majority of people's friend groupings are the result of chance and momentum. With so much at stake, selecting those closest to you should be an extremely thoughtful process. The chance and capacity to construct a social circle methodically will improve both your life and the lives of individuals in the circle.

The objective is to develop a social circle that is both challenging and supportive, depending on your current needs. The ideal buddy group will demonstrate that the whole is greater than the sum of its parts, with all friends progressing more readily through life, having more fun, and learning more.

**Develop Emotional Self-Sufficiency from Strangers and Friends.**

At times, we all require emotional support. Whether It is someone to sit with you and sympathize during a difficult period or someone to cheer you up when you are down in the dumps, however, it is critical to obtain that assistance from the appropriate individuals and not to put that need on others who are unwilling to fulfill it.

A friendship is similar to a savings account. The more money you invest; the more money you can withdraw. I have friends who can be miserable and unbearable for weeks at a time, and I would let them stay at my house and do whatever I could to help them reclaim their mental health. That is not something I would do for strangers. I have a lengthy and wonderful history with my friends, with so many positive memories, experiences, and feelings that they could draw from me for an extended period without feeling any sense of imposition.

Naturally, I feel the same way about my friends' support. I make an effort to require little of others, but I have a group of close friends who would gladly provide me whatever assistance I require if the need arose.

However, what happens when someone requires external assistance but lacks intimate friendships? If he is unable to resolve the issue on his own, he resorts to imposing on acquaintances. This is unpleasant not just because it imposes an obligation on the acquaintance but also because it deteriorates the relationship and reduces the probability of developing into a meaningful friendship.

A two-pronged approach is required to accomplish this goal: becoming self-sufficient enough to impose only when necessary and developing a sufficiently robust community of close friends. It is practically impossible to overdraw on the friendship bank.

A guy who is emotionally detached from acquaintances most certainly minimizes the burdens he throws on his friends. Still, he also makes it extremely easy for new individuals to become his friends by requiring little of them in the early phases of the friendship.

**It is critical to be able to manage oneself socially in every scenario.**

As with the ability to relate to people from different social strata, it is critical to manage oneself in every social setting that may happen. An excellent litmus test is for someone to feel comfortable introducing you to any of his friends or inviting you to any event.

For instance, are you capable of fending for yourself if you are dropped into a party? Can you initiate discussions with strangers and be a beneficial influence without your friend introducing you and ensuring your well-being?

What if you are forced to speak with someone you dislike? Can you be relied upon to remain respectful, avoid alienating them, and possibly even benefit them? What if everyone at the party agrees to go to a restaurant that serves meals that you dislike? Will you accompany them and make the best of the situation?

This is critical because it directly impacts the quality and number of introductions you receive, which will almost certainly be a key source of information for your social life. If the introducer is certain that you will be an asset in any setting, even if you do not connect with the person he is presenting you to, you will receive a lot more introductions.

Additionally, suppose you are not concerned with the context of your conversations and are only comfortable in particular locations. In that case, that's one degree of anxiety that won't come in the way of your interactions with others.

**People will develop a greater fondness for you as they learn more about you.**

While first impressions are critical and will be discussed in detail, it is your lingering influence that will decide the depth of your friendships. To develop exceptional friendships and maximize the likelihood that casual acquaintances will become good friends, you must be the type of person who improves with time.

We all know someone who is the polar opposite. They're enjoyable in large numbers since you can converse for a few minutes with them, but two hours with them would drive you insane. It is heartbreaking to see folks like them occasionally because you know they're decent people with good intentions and much to contribute, but their social skills alienate others.

You want to believe that anyone would like you if they spent enough time with you in an ideal world. This isn't even a stretch; It is the first step. Increase your social strengths and eliminate your deficiencies, and you will be there.

If you do not already have this, you will want to pay close attention to the sections of the book devoted to overcoming social shortcomings. If you are a decent person with some unique life experiences, which I am assuming you are, you are long-term likable. If you discover that people are unwilling to go the extra mile to befriend you, it is likely because you are making some easily correctable social errors that drive them away.

# Chapter 2: Getting Started with the Process

As you attempt to enhance your social skills, it is critical that you approach the process appropriately. Many people struggle with social skills development not because they face insurmountable obstacles but because they approach the process incorrectly and become excessively disheartened. You will make greater progress if you have the proper mindset, expectations, and approach to improvement. This chapter discusses some points you should be aware of before beginning to work on your concerns. This chapter also addresses some of the most often asked questions and concerns about enhancing one's social skills.

**Identifying which skills and characteristics to improve and which to leave alone**

As stated earlier, you do not need to alter your personality to improve your social skills drastically. Of course, you will want to address the obvious issues that most people would like to overcome—shyness and anxiety, low self-esteem, unrefined conversation skills, and a lack of understanding about how to make friends.

The characteristics listed below can also contribute to social difficulties. They are all entirely acceptable deviations from the norm, and you should not be required to adjust them. They can, however, pose real social difficulties if people misinterpret and look down on the features or if the traits cause you to have conflicting demands.

**Acceptable, if occasionally unworkable, social characteristics**

- Possessing an introverted personality
- Spending much time alone
- Not requiring or desiring a huge number of friends

- Being selective in who you associate with.

- Prefer to socialize for shorter periods before returning home to recharge your batteries; being drained by socializing

- Prefer low-key socializing and avoiding rowdy parties or getting drunk

- Prefer to sit back and listen more in conversations rather than talking a lot and attempting to be the center of attention

- Preference for substantive conversations

- Participation in "uncool," non-mainstream activities

- Disinterest in allegedly popular pursuits such as team sports or reality television

- Adherence to an unusual way of life or being part of a non-mainstream scene or subculture

For instance, having unconventional hobbies may work against you if they force your peers to stereotype you and dismiss you without giving you a chance. Your desire to spend time alone may collide with your social objectives. While a part of you may like to socialize more, your desire to spend time alone may get in the way.

You will need to determine how to approach your permissible disparities in light of your social objectives. Wherever feasible, you should be true to yourself and seek out your specialty, including companions who understand and appreciate your uniqueness.

Nobody is socially flawless. They can still survive as long as they bring enough good to the table. If you come across a piece of advice in this book that you are unsure about adopting, consider the following:

"Would omitting this specific characteristic make me happy in the long run? Could I cope with the penalties of not adhering to it?" For instance, perhaps you are comfortable with a more direct communication style and can deal with the knowledge that it may occasionally annoy others. Perhaps you will even decide that you are alright with certain features of your modest shyness, even if they are technically an "issue." Decide for yourself what works for you.

At times, you may analyze the advantages and disadvantages and decide that adhering to particular social customs is in your best interest. For instance, you would never give fashion a second thought in your ideal world, but you recognize that others do, and therefore you learn to dress a little better. Or you enjoy spending time alone but force yourself to be around others slightly more than you would like to practice your social skills and spend time with your friends.

You will have to determine for yourself where you stand and what you are willing to give up. If something violates your fundamental principles or you despise it, changing is not an option. The pragmatic method may work if you are indifferent to something and it does not require much effort to accept it. However, there will always be aspects of the social environment in which you will be unable to participate, even though you understand intellectually why you should.

The majority of people are unlikely to abandon their religious or political beliefs to fit in. To use a lighter example, some men are uninterested in athletics but recognize that they would have an easier time connecting with other males if they were. While some never develop an interest in sports, they can manage to keep up with just enough news about game scores and trades to lubricate their conversations. Others cannot bring themselves to do even that and are content with the slight inconveniences that entail.

## 2.1 Improving Your Social Skills

Although you do not have to reinvent yourself or sell yourself to succeed socially entirely, as a growing teenager, it is very important that you strive to maintain an open mind. Be receptive to new experiences and the chance that you may develop characteristics or develop an appreciation for things you never imagined you would enjoy. Individuals transform their lives. It's critical to remain loyal to yourself, but not to the point of becoming stuck in your ways and dismissing everything new with "No, that's not who I am." Consider the following scenario: A friend invites you to an introductory salsa lesson, and you have never danced before. Even if you have a sense that it is not something you would benefit from, it is too stiff to say, "That is not me! I am not a dancer and never will be!" You are not obligated to try everything everyone suggests, but you never know — you may find that you enjoy partner dancing but are unaware of it.

**Recognize that your interpersonal skills do not have to be perfect to have a fulfilling social life**

Numerous people worldwide have enjoyable social lives despite being a little shy and nervous, occasionally stumbling in their interactions, lacking an abundance of exciting hobbies, or possessing a few annoying personality traits. Even the most charismatic individuals make poor jokes or have their invitations declined. You are not required to master every ability in this book 100 percent of the time, nor are you required to win the approval of every single individual on the earth. Simply being good enough to get by and having people who accept you for who you are is sufficient. You do not require that all of your encounters be flawless. You only need enough of them to go well that you can accomplish your social goals (if you invite ten people to hang out and only three accept, but they wind up becoming close friends, you have won).

**Practicing your social skills to improve them**

Social skills are no different than any other talent. While reading recommendations might help you identify areas for improvement and make the learning process go more smoothly, you must ultimately practice grasping the material truly. You have undoubtedly spent fewer hours socializing overall than many of your peers, and you will need to make up for the lost time.

That may seem self-evident, yet when it comes to interpersonal skills, some believe they can be acquired all at once by applying the appropriate trick, insight, psychology "hack," or confidence booster. They probably believe this because social skills are intangible and cliched. People intuitively recognize that developing complicated physical abilities such as skiing or sketching takes time. When it comes to socializing, their mental process is as follows: "It is merely a conversation. That is something I am already familiar with. Therefore, provide me with some top-secret, extremely effective conversation formulas, and I'll be off to the races."

Additionally, most participants felt it easier to navigate a social setting when they were briefly more confident than usual. As a result, they argue that there must be a way to maintain an elevated level of confidence at all times. However, while you can briefly experience an uncommon sense of self-assurance, there is no way to summon that sensation on command or lock it in place for good. There are truly no shortcuts. If there were, they would be widely known, and this book would be unnecessary.

**Ways to Develop your social skills**

Three ways exist for you to practice your social skills. To begin, if you believe you are socially inexperienced on a general level, you can identify strategies to increase your social interaction.

Although this method is unstructured, you will still learn new things and refine a range of skills due to the additional hours you accumulate. You may:

- Increase your social interactions with those you know (existing friends, coworkers, classmates, housemates, and family members);

- Employ yourself in a position that requires extensive engagement with others (for example, retail, restaurant waiter, bartender, call center, or sales);

- Join a volunteer role that requires interaction with others (for example, fundraising, speaking with seniors, or assisting at a festival);

- Become a member of a club, team, or organization;

- Attend online meet-ups planned by others (for example, through a forum you are enrolled in or through services such as Meetup.com);

- Utilize natural opportunities for quick, nice conversations with others who are normally expected to be cheerful and converse with you, such as store clerks and restaurant servers;

- Visit a venue that allows patrons to arrive alone and engage in social interaction with other guests (for example, a board game café, a tavern, or a pool hall);

- Communicate with other teens online (for example, chatting with people while playing a multiplayer game). Of course, technology cannot replace face-to-face practice, but it should not be discounted either; or

- Travel and stay in busy, social hostels if it is a feasible option for you.

A second strategy is to practice in a purposeful, systematic manner, particularly useful for refining specific skills. For instance, if you have difficulty initiating discussions, you may attend one online-organized meet-up every week and engage in conversation with at least five new people. If you are having difficulty with a particular form of encounter, such as inviting someone out or declining an unreasonable request, you can practice with a friend or family member. Certain organizations and counseling agencies offer social skills training groups that practice in a secure, supportive atmosphere.

**A third option** to practice social skills is to enroll in a teens training session that teaches performance-based interpersonal skills such as public speaking, acting, improvisation, or stand-up comedy. These highly specialized skills do not entirely transfer to everyday circumstances. A memorized, rehearsed speech is not the same thing as an unscripted, informal talk. Nonetheless, they provide a plethora of benefits. For instance, speech training can teach you how to project your voice and communicate with confidence through your body language. Taking part in a play may assist you in overcoming your anxiety and dread of being put on the spot. Improvisation teaches you how to be more spontaneous, loose, and playful in your conversations. Many people also experience a minor boost in their regular interactions due to gaining proficiency with a more intimidating ability, such as public speaking.

You do not have to spend a lot of time in public conversing with strangers to practice your social skills. Certain individuals believe they are obligated to engage in a random conversation with strangers at the mall or grocery store. If you are attempting to develop a habit of initiating and maintaining conversations with strangers, that's one thing. If you are looking to gain some social experience in general, conversing with strangers is typically too stressful and inefficient.

It's preferable to practice with people you already know and feel comfortable with or with strangers you meet in more structured environments, such as an art class.

**Improving your social success indirectly**

While addressing the less-practiced elements of your social skills directly is critical, you may also help your cause indirectly by being a more well-rounded, smart, and interesting person. Consider a three-month period during which you did not explicitly practice your social skills but instead traveled, discovered new music, and learned mountain biking. After those three months, you are likely to find that many social situations will go more smoothly for you. You would have more to discuss and relate to others, and you would notice a significant difference if you ended up in conversation with a traveler, cyclist, or music lover. Traveling and learning to mountain bike would have boosted your overall confidence or made you more fun and adventurous. The holiday experiences you had may have some cachet and make others want to speak with you more to understand more about them.

That does not mean that if you acquire a slew of new hobbies, you will be able to evade the requirement for direct practice. Additionally, some people who hear this advice attempt to learn everything and do everything to maximize their social advantage. Naturally, that is not practicable.

**Having an idea of how long it will take to improve your social skills.**

Of course, estimating how much time you will need to refine your social skills is difficult because everyone begins at a different point. One to three years is a reasonable amount of time to anticipate if you are behind in all areas, rather than just one or two. Generally, it takes a few years to become somewhat decent in a variety of skills.

While one to three years may seem lengthy, the process of improvement will not be monotonous throughout. As is the case with most things, it will be the most difficult at first and then become more pleasurable and comfortable once you have established a solid basis. It's similar to learning to play the guitar: for the first month, holding down the strings pains your fingers, and playing a chord properly, let alone switching between several of them swiftly and gracefully, is a feat. At the six-month mark, the situation has shifted dramatically. You are still a clueless beginning in the broad scheme of things, but you have learned enough that practicing isn't a chore and is frequently enjoyable once you have mastered a new tune. The same holds for socializing. At first, it may feel awkward to engage in polite conversation with someone for a few minutes. After a year, you may confidently attend a party with a group of friends, knowing you will get some practice socializing while having a wonderful time.

## 2.2 Some Common Challenges and Concerns

This chapter discusses major practical obstacles to developing interpersonal skills and addresses some common concerns about the process.

### Practical difficulties

Even if you desire to improve your social skills, the following obstacles may make it difficult to begin and maintain working on them. All of these obstacles are surmountable.

**"I would like to practice my social skills, but certain situations drain me quickly."**

When people socialize, it's not uncommon for them to soon become mentally exhausted. They can hold themselves for an hour or two at a dinner party conversation, but after that, they feel depleted, as if they want to leave.

They are too exhausted after a few hours to listen to everyone and construct their responses correctly. They typically require some downtime following their interactions.

Being easily frustrated can impair your capacity to practice or hang out with friends as long as you would like. From an "acceptable, but inconvenient, differences" standpoint, you may also be irritated when others do not understand why you are wired this way; some less sensitive individuals may give you a hard time if you want to leave an event early, or they may take it personally if you appear exhausted in their presence.

Another possibility is that you are underestimating your ability to progress on your own. To master any complex talent, you must occasionally be able to direct your progress. Everyone is unique, and your requirements will not always match a template. You must understand how to prioritize your efforts and create your practice exercises if none are accessible. As a result of their lack of social achievement, some individuals develop a sense of powerlessness and inactivity toward the situation. They believe, "I have no idea how to socialize. I've never been able to find out how to improve on my own. The only way I am going to have a shot is if someone holds my hand throughout." Not true. You can improve.

**Concerns regarding the prospect of honing your interpersonal skills**

Fear of being forced to change too much and sell out to improve society is a widespread issue. This book has already addressed several of these concerns, but here are a few more:

**"I am uncertain whether I want to improve my interpersonal skills. I do not lead a particularly social life, and I am content with that."**

The likelihood is that you are reading this book due to a desire to improve your social situation. Perhaps, however, you are more ambiguous.

Perhaps someone purchased this book for you, and you are casually leafing through it.

If you are content with your current social situation, this book will not attempt to change it. However, it is critical to make that choice with complete self-awareness and honesty. Anxiety, despair, and previous resentments about being singled out can all distort your motivations. You can convince yourself that you do not want something you believe you cannot have.

If you prefer to spend all of your time at home and have few friends, and you made that decision rationally, that is OK. If you believe you want to live a mostly solitary existence because a) your anxiety has gotten out of control, b) you are convinced no one would like you if you attempted to make friends, and c) you are bitter about the idea of being social because you were teased in high school for being "weird," that's another story. It's acceptable if you are not always working at 100 percent self-awareness; no one is. Check-in with yourself regularly and change your course as necessary.

**"I am unsure whether or not to focus on my social skills. I dislike socializing and see no reason to improve my skills."**

If you dislike socializing, you should live a life that reflects your personality. However, a sizable proportion of those who hold this perspective is younger. They believe they dislike socializing because they have not had the opportunity to experience how fulfilling it can be. Simply put, they are unaware of their loss. They associate the term "conversation" with all the awkward or insulting interactions they've encountered rather than with interesting, affirming exchanges with like-minded friends.

If your social skills are underdeveloped, you will have a harder time "unlocking" the pleasure in various circumstances. For instance, attending a party will feel like a chore if you cannot socialize and engage in stimulating conversations and are uncomfortable letting loose or dancing. Naturally, if you do not get much out of parties even after learning how to navigate them, that's fine as well. It's also acceptable if you are not particularly interested in developing your social skills at parties, to begin with. Not everyone must share similar interests or be a social butterfly. However, when you are inexperienced or gun-shy, your perception of how enticing different socializing forms might be clouded. When your interpersonal skills and confidence improve, you may discover that you like some activities more than you did previously.

If you were singled out for totally acceptable distinctions such as your interests, I agree that you should not be required to modify them. However, if being picked on has resulted in the development of social problems that have an undeniable detrimental impact on your life, you probably want to improve by eradicating them.

While it is unfortunate that you have encountered these challenges, they are nevertheless concerns that must be addressed. You are merely restraining yourself if you refuse to deal with them out of an irrational sense of injustice. It is like if you are strolling down the street and a stranger leaps from behind a corner and shoots you in the leg. Is this your fault? Certainly not. Is it unjust? Certainly. Is whoever committed this heinous act a bad person? Definitely. However, you still have a bullet wound in your thigh that requires attention. You cannot alter the world; you can only work on yourself.

# Chapter 3: Social Fear and Anxiety

I will be honest with you. Social relationships may cause stress at times.

The act of connecting with others is meant to be social. However, it may be tough to enjoy social encounters if you are suffering from anxiety. Fortunately, there is a method for overcoming your fear. While you will not be able to remove fear entirely, you can keep it from taking over your life.

To do so, you must first recognize the difference between true fear and physical fear.

## 3.1 Physical Fear vs. True Fear

True fear is a good thing. It is your body's method of warning you of impending danger. If a bear wanders into your campsite, you will get an adrenaline rush, your heart will start to pound, and your mind will start shouting, "THAT IS A BEAR!". Due to your fear, you will leave all else you are doing and strive to defend yourself. Genuine fear is used by your body to keep you safe from true danger.

When your body initiates the fear response despite the lack of a real threat, this is known as physical fear. You could have the same bodily reaction to a monster in a horror film as you did to the bear at your campsite. The difference is that a bear can hurt you, while special effects cannot.

Your body is unable to differentiate between the two. You, on the other hand, can do so.

You can appreciate a horror movie if you know the difference between a reasonably harmless movie creature and a real-life bear danger. Learning to differentiate between physical fear and genuine fear might also help you gain from social encounters. Take a moment to consider this. In social situations, your fear is almost entirely physical, not genuine fear. You may be concerned that you may say or do something offensive, causing others to humiliate you or pass judgment on you.

But here's the thing: do you know what? Almost none of these things are likely going to happen. And even if it does happen, it is not a big deal.

Say it out loud with me.

It is all right.

## 3.2 Social Anxiety = Physical Fear

What if you are having a conversation with somebody and say something awkward?

You are going to feel uneasy. The other person may grow furious or laugh at you. You will, however, recover. The discussion will change to a new topic, and the other person will soon forget about your humiliation.

In the worst-case situation, you will try again with another individual in a new conversation.

There has been no actual harm.

A bear did not maul anyone.

Failure is not meant to be a big deal when it comes to social connections.

Reread what you just read.

Failure is not a major concern.

There will be no long-term consequences if you mess up in a single social contact.

Take some deep breaths and tell yourself that a bear has ever attacked no one before starting a new conversation.

There is, however, an exception to this principle.

If you offend or upset someone with whom you have a long-term connection (such as a long-time companion or friend), you may face severe penalties because you may jeopardize your relationship. However, to do long-term harm, you must significantly upset or offend someone, which is unlikely to happen if you strive to be sensitive to their feelings.

Furthermore, your most serious anxiety is generally caused by people you do not know well.

There is no relationship to endanger and hence no genuine danger when you do not know someone well.

**Fear-free living**

As a result, the next time your anxiety rises at the possibility of social interaction, convince yourself that it is merely physical fear.

Even if you make a mistake, social interaction is unlikely to hurt you. I am well aware that this reminder will not affect physical fear. It is possible that your heart may continue to race, and your hands will continue to sweat. You will, however, have the energy and motivation to face your fears.

Conquering fear is, of course, a process.

If you have a social anxiety condition or have experienced severe bullying and rejection, your fear may be extremely strong. And if that is the case, that is OK. I do not expect someone to read this book and immediately lose their fear. Rather, I hope this book inspires you to take small, steady movements away from your fears.

Choose a goal that looks terrifying but is doable, and use your understanding of true fear and physical fear to help you achieve it.

Failure is not a huge issue, so do not be alarmed if you fail the first time you try to achieve the objective. Furthermore, do not feel compelled to do this work on your own. If possible, enlist the help of family and friends or join a support group to help you along your way.

As I have mentioned, counselors may be helpful, and there is no shame in consulting with one.

It is important to remember that anxiety is a condition that may be conquered. You can overcome anxiety, but it will take time and may require the help of friends, counselors, and loved ones. Simply make little, steady steps toward your goal, and remember that you do not have to be afraid of failure, despite what physical fear may tell you.

Be brave.

## 3.3 True Intimacy vs. Manipulation

So, there is a quick rundown of what I aim to do here (and what I am not).

My goal is to lay a solid basis for social skills that will allow you to form deep, fulfilling, and real friendships.

I am not claiming to teach you all there is to know about social skills or to turn you into a social superhero.

I just want you to have the skills you need to build great connections.

The problem is that these skills can be misused. Martin Luther King Jr. was a gifted orator, but so was Adolf Hitler too. The idea of utilizing social skills to deceive or persuade people to give you what you want may be quite enticing.

There are also many "gurus" of social skills who preach a philosophy of deceit and manipulation. They promise to teach social skills that can help you gain power and influence, persuade people to follow your wishes, and achieve your desires. Many practical challenges arise from these

manipulation-based social skills (most strategies fail to work or operate only in a few constrained circumstances).

Furthermore, they are both immoral and false.

Most people reading this guide, I believe, are as devoted as I am to building relationships based on trust and respect rather than manipulation and dishonesty.

If such is the case, you may safely skip this section.

A word of warning, though, for those lured by the prospect of manipulation:

## 3.4 Manipulation Is Dangerous

Productive partnerships are built on mutual respect and trust. When you manipulate someone, you immediately demean them and destroy their trust in you. You may get what you want in the short term by deceit and manipulation, but your dishonesty will always be exposed in the long run.

You will never get the true intimacy you want through deceit.

So, if you want to learn how to persuade people to do what you want, attract women, or build a false image of yourself to deceive others, this book is not for you.

But here's the thing:

You do not need manipulation or deceit. The aim of this book is that you do not have to change who you are to be loved or accepted. I feel that allowing others to get to know you will result in good connections genuinely. You do not have to sway someone's opinion or mislead them about your true identity. All you have to do now is give them the chance to get to know you.

It is challenging to participate in discussions that allow others to know you if you lack good social skills. On the other hand, social skills may be learned (which is why this book exists!).

Your true personality will emerge once a lack of social skills no longer constrains you.

That is a worthy goal to strive for.

Refuse to give up and refuse to settle.

# Chapter 4: Empathy

Empathy is the ability to see the world through the eyes of another. Empathy refers to the capacity to comprehend what another person is feeling at any given moment and why their actions make sense to them.

Empathy enables us to convey our thoughts in a way that makes sense to others and enables us to comprehend people when they communicate with us. It is one of the fundamental building blocks of great social connection and, quite obviously, powerful stuff.

However, how do you develop empathy? How do you comprehend what another person is feeling if this does not happen automatically?

To some level, we are all predisposed to sympathize with others. Our brains are wired to perceive the emotions of others. That is why we feel bad when someone gets hurt or why we are more inclined to laugh if someone else is laughing as well. An outstanding book on this subject called Social Intelligence details all of the data that supports this natural empathy.

Regrettably, only a few people are born with exceptional innate empathy. Our empathetic wiring is continuous. Specific individuals possess remarkable natural empathy and can tell how another person is feeling by looking at them. Certain people are born with a minuscule degree of natural empathy, and they will not notice you are furious until you start yelling. Most people fall somewhere in the middle, understanding how another person feels only some of the time.

Fortunately, empathy is a combination of natural ability and training. Depending on your initial level of skill, improving your empathy may need more or less effort than it does for someone else - but regardless of your starting point, you can teach yourself to be more empathic.

And this part is here to educate you how.

Empathy teaches three lessons:

**Self-Awareness**

If you wish to comprehend the emotions of others, you must first learn to empathize with yourself. "Self-Awareness" has been written to assist you in understanding and accepting your feelings. Understanding and accepting one's own emotions is critical for a healthy life and serves as the foundation for empathizing with others.

**Understanding Others**

Anyone can develop an understanding of how others think and feel through practice and a commitment to contemplation. Understanding Others is the blueprint that demonstrates how.

**Nonverbal Empathy**

When you comprehend what another person is thinking or experiencing, it becomes easier to interact with them. However, there is a nonverbal component to an interaction that demands special attention. Empathy-based knowledge can assist you in employing proper nonverbal communication. Nonverbal Empathy explains how.

# 4.1 Self-Awareness

Empathy is a critical trait for social interactions. If you understand what other people are thinking and experiencing, you can be a better friend and have more effective interactions.

However, to develop empathy for others, you must first develop empathy for yourself.

That sounds highly sentimental to you as a teen but bear with me. This is critical and practical. Learning to empathize with yourself entails comprehending and accepting what you feel and why you are feeling it.

If you are furious, you should be able to recognize the phrase "I am angry," as well as the grounds for your anger. You should be comfortable with experiencing your emotions rather than ignoring or suppressing them.

Fundamentally, if something genuinely hurtful occurs to you, it should be acceptable for you to be sad. You should allow yourself to be sad. Occasionally, we develop the belief that we must always appear joyful or that our issues are trivial compared to others and hence feel self-centered when we are unhappy or upset.

However, this is not true. Your troubles are significant because you are significant. And if anything happens that hurts you or makes you unhappy, it is okay to express your unhappiness and allow yourself to experience it. You are not required to keep that pent up.

**Acceptance of One's Emotions**

Of course, it is an excellent idea to improve your position so that whatever is causing you to feel sad no longer does. You are not obligated to be depressed.

And, while everyone feels unhappy or furious at times, you should consider seeing a counselor if you feel this way all the time. Just like a doctor may assist you in healing medically, a counselor can assist you in healing emotionally, and there is no shame in speaking with one.

By the way, this is true for more than simply emotional comprehension. Consult a counselor if you are battling despair, anxiety, loneliness, or any number of other issues. There is no shame in it, and it may just transform or save your life.

However, the point is that you should allow yourself to experience your feelings. It is acceptable to be sad if anything awful happens to you. You should feel safe communicating your feelings to friends and family, especially if you are not feeling well or are unsure why you think the way you do. Fundamentally, you should understand that your emotions are a part of you, and just as you must accept yourself, you must accept your emotions.

Take a moment to reread that paragraph. No, truly. Reread it. I am going to wait.

**Recognize your emotions.**

Consider whether these statements are true for you. Are you aware of the source of your emotions when you experience them? Do you give yourself permission to feel an emotion? Accept that it is okay to feel the way you do? Do you have a healthy outlet for your feelings?

If the response to any of those questions is "No" or "I am not sure," then take some time to consider how you feel. Consider why you are responding in that manner and what you need to improve your empathy for yourself. Speak with someone you trust, solicit their advice and support, or consider scheduling an appointment with a counselor.

It may take some time to go through this, but the time commitment is well worth it. Having a healthy and robust awareness of your own emotions enables you to live a happy, healthy life. Humans are emotional beings, and your emotions are an integral part of who you are.

And, of course, emotions are a part of everyone else. If you understand what it is like to experience an emotion, you will be better equipped to comprehend and communicate with someone experiencing something similar. Therefore, even if you do not wish to understand your emotions for your own sake, do so to benefit your relationships with others. It is worthwhile.

**Thinking It Through**

Today, I would like you to complete an activity. It may seem strange at first, but trust me, I believe you will find it quite beneficial.

As you go about your day, keep an eye on your emotions and look for instances when you are experiencing something (whether it is annoyance, happiness, sadness, boredom, or anything else). Then, take some time to consider why you are feeling that way.

I want you to delve under the surface here. It is natural to be outraged when someone cuts you off in traffic and says, "Well, I am angry because I got cut off." However, if you dig a little deeper, you may discover that you are angry because the other driver mistreated you, and you frequently lack respect in your other relationships. Alternatively, you may feel furious because you are in pain due to a difficult period in your life but are refusing to acknowledge it. You may even realize that you have no legitimate reason to be furious, at which point your anger will subside.

Consider your emotions in whatever way is most comfortable for you. Perhaps you could schedule some time at the end of the day to go for a walk to provide yourself with some quiet time to contemplate. Maybe you could jot down your ideas about your feelings for the day and then compare your notes from different days to look for trends. Alternatively, you could ask a friend or family member to assist you with comprehending your emotions and discussing them with your loved ones.

Whatever the outcome, I believe you will discover that you gain a greater understanding of yourself, which will make it easier to understand others. Give it a shot. And after you feel like you are beginning to understand your own emotions, continue reading to learn how to understand the feelings of others.

## 4.2 Understanding Others

Previously, we discussed how to empathize with yourself. Empathizing with yourself enables you to empathize with others, as understanding your feelings makes it simpler to understand the sentiments of others.

However, if you genuinely wish to understand others, you will require more than self-empathy. Additionally, you should spend some time considering how other people perceive the world.

This may sound difficult, but it boils down to one thing:

Train yourself to pose the question "How does this scenario appear to the other person?" during each conversation, and invest the brain cycles to come up with a reasonable response.

The objective here is not to be a mind reader or know precisely what the other person is thinking. All you have to do is envision what it would be like to be that person and make educated guesses about what that person is thinking or feeling.

**Empathy and the Art of Sock Collecting**

For instance, suppose a friend approaches you and begins conversing about a subject you find unbearably boring (their sock collection, perhaps).

If you view the scenario through your own eyes, you will likely become upset and snap at your friend. They should have realized how uninteresting socks are to you!

However, if you take the time to view it from the friend's perspective, you gain a deeper understanding of their behavior. Most likely, if the individual is a friend, they genuinely care about you and are not attempting to bore you. Most likely, in their excitement to tell someone about their new alpaca wool crew socks, they forgot how dull socks are to you.

From your vantage point, you have been sucked into a boring conversation. From their perspective, they are sharing something exciting with you.

Once you have taken the time to consider the situation from their perspective, you will handle it much more effectively. You will not snap at them now that you have realized they are not trying to bore you.

Other than that, you could attempt to change the conversation gently. Alternatively, you may determine that this is an opportunity to strengthen your friendship with your friend and utilize the conversation to learn more about something (socks!) that is meaningful to them.

**The Peril of Your Perspective**

Unfortunately, our natural propensity is to observe things from our perspective (thus the name OUR perspective.)

Rather than attempting to understand how the other person sees things, we try to persuade them to view things our way. Rather than understanding that the other person will always see things differently, we become irritated with them for not seeing things the way we do.

I used to be constantly guilty of this. I would do or say something rude to my parents to enrage them. Then I would become enraged with them for being enraged with me!

I had no intention of being disrespectful, and as a result, I grew incensed when they accused me of being disrespectful-it seemed as though my motivations should have been evident to them!

**Discipline Is Required**

Once I began to develop empathy, everything changed. I began to wonder, "Why are my parents so upset?" And when I reflected on that question, I realized that even though I did not intend to disrespect, my parents felt disrespected. My parents are lovely people, but they are not mind readers, so they cannot understand my motivations, only my actions.

Once I recognized this, I was much better equipped to resolve our arguments constructively. When I considered doing an action, I asked myself, "How would this appear to my parents?" This helped me avoid saying or doing something that would anger my parents. Our friendship strengthened, and confrontation with my parents became far less frequent.

I provide this anecdote to emphasize a critical aspect. When someone does something that appears nonsensical to you, it makes perfect sense to them. If you take a step back and ask, "Okay, why is this individual behaving this way?" you will typically discover a plausible explanation, which can help you respond more effectively.

However, asking that question does not occur automatically. You must make a conscious choice to question yourself, "How does this appear to the other person?" You must be willing to relinquish your insistence that the other person views things your way. And you must repeat this process often until it becomes instinctive.

**Importance of True Empathy**

Empathy is not easy to develop. I will admit this.

However, when you continue to ask yourself, "How does this circumstance appear to the other person?" Something extraordinary will occur. The question itself will become increasingly irrelevant. You will have an intuitive understanding of what the other person is experiencing.

In other words, you will begin to develop genuine empathy.

This does require time. You have spent a long time viewing the world purely through your lens and hence will need to undo years of habit. However, believe me when I say that it is well worth the effort.

I have also got an exercise for you today. You may find it challenging at first, but it will jump-start your ability to develop empathy for others. The following is the exercise:

Consider the following questions when you engage in conversations today: "What is the other person thinking and feeling right now? How do they see this interaction?" Of course, you may never know for sure whether your guess is correct, but more often than not, you will be close.

Once you feel comfortable asking that question, determine whether you are capable of acting on that understanding. Perhaps the grocery store clerk says, "Hello," in a monotone voice, and you think, "Gosh, this person has been working all day and is feeling worn out." Therefore, check if you can cheer them up! Inform them that they are doing an excellent job, compliment them on their smile, or inquire about the source of their earrings.

Developing a sense of familiarity with this will take time, but it will become easier with each repetition. Once you gain empathy for others, it will become easy to demonstrate empathy to them.

## 4.3 Nonverbal Empathy

When you inquire into what other people are thinking and feeling, you obtain insight into the most effective way to communicate with them. This understanding enables you to diffuse disagreement and steer the discourse.

There is also a nonverbal component to responding to empathy. If you see a buddy is upset yet ask, "What is wrong?" in a pleasant tone, your friend may believe you do not care. However, if you adjust your tone to appear empathetic and concerned, your friend will likely assume you want to know what is wrong. As you may recall, your words and nonverbal cues work together to communicate, and you want them to be in sync.

Now that I think about it, I realize I have already given you a lot to work on. Empathy will eventually become second nature to you, but it can take considerable effort to train yourself to be aware of what the other person is thinking and feeling. When combined with the requirement to manage one's nonverbal cues, empathy might appear overpowering.

However, do not worry. Nonverbal empathy is relatively simple. Similar to how body language is reduced to two signals, there are just two nonverbal empathy options to consider: high or low energy.

What do I mean by high- and low-energy?

**Definition of High and Low Energy**

When someone is brimming with vitality, they tend to act ecstatic, expressive, and loud. In comparison, when someone is low on energy, they tend to act erratically reserved, relaxed and quiet.

Take note that high energy does not always equal happiness, and low energy does not always equal sadness. Someone who has just won the lottery may get up and celebrate, or they may lean back in their chair with a gradual, contented smile growing across their face. Both are positive answers, but one is high-energy while the other is low-energy.

Additionally, keep in mind that people will experience periods of high and low energy. When you witness a buddy having a good time, you should conclude, "My friend is having a good time right now," rather than concluding, "My friend is always having a good time."

**Empathy and Vitality**

The concept of high- and low-energy is straightforward. However, how does this connect to empathy?

If your companion is energetic, strive to be energetic and if your partner is a low-energy person, strive to be a low-energy person.

That is what I mean.

Assume you are meeting a friend for supper. Your friend has had a full day, and you notice they are less loud than usual. They are experiencing a lack of energy.

On the other hand, you are ecstatic with the restaurant. As a result, you brag about the cuisine and ambiance, flirt with the wait staff, and generally behave expressive and excited. Meanwhile, your companion picks at her food and wishes you would calm down so she could have a peaceful talk with you.

In other words, you are high-energy, whereas your friend is low-energy. Your companion desires a calm evening while you wish to party and be crazy. Because there is a mismatch, it makes it more difficult for you to connect with your companion.

## Matching Nonverbal Energy

However, if you match your energy level to your friend's, the evening will go much more smoothly. When you see your friend is low on energy, you can act more restrained and calmer, even though you feel thrilled. Alternatively, if you see your friend as a high-energy person, you might respond by being more excited and active.

Keep in mind that you should match, not exceed, your partner's energy level. If your partner is easygoing and tranquil, you should be similarly low-energy, but there is no need to act like Eeyore. If your companion is noisy and loud, you should be as well, but there is no need to go wild.

Energy matching applies to social circumstances as well as to individuals. For example, a formal event is likely to be low-energy (so it is prudent to be solemn and reserved, even if you are excited). In contrast, a party is expected to be high-energy (so it is prudent to be more expressive and spirited, even if you are relaxed.) When entering a social event for the first time, please take a moment to assess the scenario's energy level and then utilize it to guide your own.

Of course, your energy level is also critical. It is acceptable to express your high- or low-energy state, even if your spouse is experiencing the opposite. However, it is prudent to begin by matching your energy level to that of your spouse and then returning to your natural energy level. This enables your partner to move energy levels along with you.

When you monitor the energy levels of individuals around you and change your energy level accordingly, connecting with others becomes a lot easier. Additionally, you are practicing being aware of what others are thinking and experiencing, which will help you with your general study of empathy.

As you develop empathy, you will notice that you can better comprehend others, have fewer disagreements, and form stronger relationships. That is a prize well worth the effort.

# Chapter 5: Improving Your Communication Skills

When you examine most successful professionals and leaders, one of their characteristics is the skill to communicate efficiently. This emphasizes the critical nature of communication skills and how having good communication skills can help you achieve success in your social and professional life.

## 5.1 Levels of Communication

Only two wires travel through the cable that enters your home for television. The wire, in and of itself, is a simple piece of technology that everybody can understand. However, hundreds of channels and access to the entire internet are conveyed via this seemingly simple medium.

This is a fairly comparable to the way we communicate with others. While our words may appear straightforward, they involve the transmission of multiple channels of communication simultaneously. To master social skills, you must be aware of these channels, capable of communicating effectively through them, and capable of comprehending the information provided to you via them.

**Four major channels of communication are active at all times: content, meta, emotion, and status.**

When we discuss communication superficially, we refer to **content**. If you tell me you are going to the store, the content channel simply communicates that you are going to the store.

The **meta** channel serves as the conversation's undertone. It is the inference that lies beneath the meaning. If we have been discussing how I would like to eat brownies and you are going to the store, the meta channel communication is that you are going to get the ingredients to bake me brownies. Although meta can occasionally be read independently, it is frequently contextualized.

The **emotion** channel is a passive signal rather than an active one. As we speak, those of us who are not skilled poker players are continuously leaking our emotions. "I am going to the store" is a phrase that can be spoken in various tones and cadences. You could signal that you were going to the store out of resignation because I would continue to bug you about making my brownies. You may imply that you adored me by purchasing ingredients to cook brownies for me. Additionally, you could express frustration, nervousness, excitement, or any other variety of emotions.

Finally, the **status** channel is always broadcasting information regarding our relative status. If I were your boss and directed you to prepare brownies, you could say, "I am going to the store," indicating that you understood my command and would carry it out. You may even say it in a patronizing tone, implying that you will do it because I am so far beneath you that I am incapable of performing such a simple task.

"I am going to the store," five whole words picked at random that can mean almost anything even though the content remains constant. If you were not previously in awe of communication's power, this might do the trick. It is amazing how much information can be given at the same time.

A master of communication must be capable of engaging in two extensive discussions (content and meta) while simultaneously maintaining two lesser dialogues (emotion and status).

This is a not-so-embellished statement. If someone were to transcribe your meta-conversation with another person, the transcription should be completely coherent. The other two are identical. If the conversation did not flow as effortlessly as the content channel, one or both of you would find it aggravating, even if you could not put your finger on why.

## 5.2 Make Yourself Stand Out

Once you are introduced to someone or placed in a social environment where people are unfamiliar with you, your initial objective should be to convey what makes you unique and interesting as fast as possible. While it is necessary to get to know others and contribute to making interactions more fascinating and enjoyable for everyone else, your priority should be to let them know who you are. First impressions are formed rapidly and last as subconscious biases for a long time.

Because people make snap judgments, you want to maximize the likelihood that they will regard you favorably. They share more of themselves with those they believe deserve their friendship, and only on an equal footing can you contribute to the interaction's improvement.

Your worth must be genuine and honest. That is to say, exaggerating is not a good idea. When individuals have a limited number of data points from which to judge you, each one will be significantly weighted to mean more than it does. Therefore, if you exaggerate once or say anything that does not seem to fit your personality, it will be noted and used against you.

Bragging is worse than exaggeration. Any level of boasting will negate any positive message you may have sent. Therefore, the trick is to express as much information about oneself as possible without boasting or bragging.

As a result, you will want to place a greater emphasis on who you are than on what you have done. And you want this information to be second-order, which means that a reasonable person should be able to infer characteristics about you based on what you say.

For instance, suppose you founded a business and recently achieved a million dollars in revenue. That is something to be proud of, but there is no way to bring it up without appearing to be bragging. However, you might discuss your various productivity tactics. Individuals may conclude from your techniques that you are motivated and productive, which is a positive trait in practically any social circle.

Similarly, you would not want to discuss how you go to exotic areas, but you may provide a tip for obtaining seat upgrades or tell a humorous travel story. People will infer from your non-bragging and real anecdotes that you are adventurous and enjoy traveling.

Additionally, you can convey value by asking questions. If you know an expert in a particular field, you could pose a question that assumes a certain level of understanding. While it would be rude to come out and proclaim, "Hey folks, I am a pilot!" if you flew airplanes, you might inquire someone who flew helicopters about the distinct differences between the two.

You will see that these substitutes are also more beneficial to the listener. Rather than simply impressing, they educate, entertain, or engage. If you are unsure if you are bragging or not, refrain from saying it. Bragging is incredibly destructive, and there will be several other opportunities to communicate worth. The value you are attempting to portray is those characteristics about yourself that contribute to your curiosity and pleasantness as a person.

You want to create fascination without coming off as arrogant, and you want to demonstrate that you are socially skilled, self-sufficient, and will benefit the person or group with whom you are conversing.

A sense of humor is quite valuable. Not everyone is amusing, and not everyone should be, but you may express a great deal of value through comedy if you are. Every social group takes pleasure in laughing and socializing. There are situations when joking around is inappropriate, but those situations are rarely when meeting someone for the first time. Even if a person or group believes you are worthless except for the fact that you make them laugh, they will almost certainly want you around.

Consider what makes you unique as a friend, and every time you find yourself in a new social scenario, consider which of your assets will be most valued by that group and focus on communicating them. Carry out this task early in the encounter and then get to know the other participants.

## 5.3 Eliminate the Annoyance

Before focusing on contributing significantly as a friend and member of a friend group, it is critical to address annoyance-causing behaviors. While none of us will ever eliminate our unpleasant tendencies, there is a level that must be crossed for individuals with other viable options to choose you as a friend.

This is a harsh statement, yet it is not untrue. Some people you will wish to become friends with will already have a slew of wonderful friends vying for their attention. If you have irritating tendencies, there is no assurance that a new friend or acquaintance will see past them and appreciate your positive aspects.

Another extremely irritating behavior is making poor jokes. Nobody believes they make poor jokes, yet everyone knows someone who does, indicating an evident discrepancy. Certain individuals constantly make poor jokes without realizing it. You may be one of these individuals.

Both are unpleasant characteristics, not because they indicate malice or something negative about you, but because they impose an unnecessary burden on the other person, compelling him to either deceive you or be rude.

If you speak to me excessively about issues in which I am uninterested, I must be polite, listen, and pretend interest. The only other option is for me to be impolite, either by suddenly shifting the subject or by telling you I am not interested. Certain individuals are so naïve to over talking that they will miss any slightest indications.

If your jokes are awful, you force me to either laugh and fool you or not laugh and alert you to the fact that your jokes are not funny. In any case, you have imposed an awkward imposition on me, diminishing my comfort, decreasing my interest in the conversation, and increasing my motivation to quit.

It is more difficult to identify irritating habits than it is to eliminate them. Often, awareness generates sufficient social pressure to diminish the irritating tendency. If a friend or family member is prepared to be entirely honest with you, you can question them about your irritating habits. Do not inquire as to whether you have any; simply assume that you do and inquire about what they are. This avoids the unpleasant situation of your friend revealing to you that you have some.

Consider how frequently you would be wrong in pointing out another person's irritating habit. It is probably rare to never, so presume that they are correct when someone provides you with that type of feedback.

You will, however, have to discover certain vexing habits on your own. The biggest red flag is when you repeatedly receive responses that are inconsistent with your expectations. You tell a joke, and the audience is silent. You are discussing something quite intriguing to you, but you notice that your listeners' eyes are wandering and that they do not offer to clarify questions.

These are just two of several examples. Others include excessive use of certain phrases, needless hand gestures, lack of eye contact, and a failure to listen.

## 5.4 Keep it Short and Sweet

When you start a conversation with a new individual, you should have an unwritten rule that you will do the most of the talking. If the individual is not socially skilled and is at a loss for words, this will not be an issue, as you will fill any pause with amusing anecdotes, questions, and observations.

Eventually, you want to reduce the ratio to preferably fifty-fifty. If you have a truly timid individual, you may constantly be at sixty or seventy percent. Still, anything more than that is a lecture, not a conversation, and the other person is very likely to feel annoyed.

Most people are courteous and will generally enable you to control them and dominate the conversation socially. That is not to say, however, that it is a good thing to do. This results in circumstances when you believe a conversation went quite well, but the other person never expresses an interest in hanging out.

So how do you tell if you are excessively chatty or if the other person is simply shy? You should be on the lookout for various indicators if you speak more than 50% of the time.

The first red flag is if you know that the other person is an extrovert who enjoys conversation. If he has not requested an explanation and you speak more than 50% of the time, you are making a mistake.

If the other person provides brief responses or constantly repeats the same response, he is uninterested in the conversation. For instance, if his input is a simple "yes" or "nice," but he never invests in a longer response, he probably expects you to stop speaking. A stimulating conversation will almost certainly elicit follow-up inquiries or a counter-argument. If you do not receive one of those items, remain vigilant.

Perhaps the most concerning warning sign is when someone never asks you a question. When people want to hear more from you, they ask questions. When they want less, they stop asking questions. If you seldom receive inquiries, the other person is generally scared that you will continue to speak if you begin answering.

Never, ever over-explain. If you are discussing anything cerebral, provide only the bare minimum of explanation. Proceed to your next point as soon as someone nods or agrees with something you say. When explaining, the question and answer format is optimal. It enables the person receiving the information to obtain precisely the information he requires, and it reassures the information provider that his contribution is valued.

If you are sharing a lengthy story or providing a lengthy explanation, incorporate numerous pauses. The best stories and explanations hold the audience spellbound, fearful of speaking, and missing something. If the silences remain unfilled, you can be certain that the individual is paying attention to what you have to say.

If he asks questions, that is also OK. However, if he changes the subject or reduces the complexity of the conversation, he is most likely seeking an exit.

While it is entirely OK to enjoy conversing, keep in mind that you will not truly be heard unless the other person is receptive. Utilize natural cues to ascertain his level of interest and adjust your communication accordingly. Over a longer period, combine that ability with practice presenting captivating stories to avoid people feeling like you are speaking for a long time.

## 5.5 Learn to respond properly

While speaking with someone, you should pay close attention to their responses. This is not to stroke your ego or humiliate yourself but to empower you to take ownership of the conversation and provide the other person with the experience they desire.

While gauging, it is critical to use a sliding scale that takes the context and setting of the conversation into account. For instance, if you meet someone at a common friend's party, they are extremely likely to appear more interested in your conversation than they actually are. Therefore, if they appear to be a five on a one to ten scale of interest, they may be a zero plus five politeness points.

In that situation, you should stop mid-story and see whether they invite you to continue. If they did not, their seeming degree of interest was lower. If they do ask you to continue, it indicates that they were intrigued. Occasionally, you cannot tell since a five and a zero may appear identical. Of course, there are moments when the scales tip in the opposite direction. Certain individuals exhibit little emotion or conduct badly when they exhibit excessive enthusiasm.

A friend's girlfriend may soften her comments to avoid the appearance of flirting with you, leading you to believe she was more interested in the things you brought up than she appeared to be.

This is critical since interactions should include an element of feedback. You make a statement, narrate a narrative, pose a question, and then assess the reaction. That statement or question should serve as a guide for future decisions. Too frequently, people fail to change their judgments based on external conditions and continue chatting about something boring merely to be polite. While discussing issues that interest you can be enjoyable, you will accomplish more harm than good if the other person is uninterested in the subject.

## 5.6 Keep the Conversations Alive and Engaging

Numerous social skills focus on delivering the experience desired by the other person most seamlessly and naturally possible. A significant part of this is ensuring that the topics you discuss are ones about which the other person is interested in conversing.

The simplest method to accomplish this is to drop conversational hooks and enable the other person to pick up on those that engage him. This is not a one-time technique but a framework for ongoing talks.

Coming up with conversational subjects is one of the most unpleasant aspects of socializing, especially with someone new. If your companion feels like they have to wrack their brains for discussion topics, they will have a strong incentive to exit the conversation.

In an ideal case, you present them with a natural selection of subjects to discuss and continue to add to that list as the conversation progresses. Instead of the terror that occurs when the topics run out, your partner will feel that there is an abundance of material to discuss and not enough time to cover it all. That is a far superior problem to have.

A sub goal of any conversation early in a relationship is to provide as much truthful information about yourself as possible. The more context someone has, the more value they will derive from each piece of information you provide. Even if they are not picked up, dropping hooks provide additional opportunities for fish to engage with you.

Avoid boasting when dropping hooks. The hooks should always be neutral or slightly positive; they should never be monumental achievements. Leading someone to a topic that makes you look good is a risky thing to do, as it appears as though you are bragging. If you are going to do it, you want to leave the fewest possible bragging hints. Therefore, you would never say, "When I ran a marathon," but you may add, "When I was jogging."

Additionally, do not be concerned if your hooks are not being picked up. There are a million possible explanations for this, and only one of them is that you are a boring person with no intriguing ideas. Much more likely is that they are unwilling to change the subject or have not yet heard an engaging hook to which they can say something.

# Chapter 6: Everlasting Skills to Create an Influence

In this chapter, we will be discussing the three basic skills every teen needs to learn to create an ongoing and everlasting influence. You need to become more desirable and likable to become socially successful. Everyone will love you if you are fun, and everyone will follow you if you are assertive. Let's take a deeper look at these skills.

## 6.1 Being Likeable

As previously stated, your interactions will be shaped by your comfort level, speaking abilities, and overall personality. One characteristic that affects how much others like your company is your likeability. People are aware of this and frequently inquire about how they might improve their likability. Although the phrase appears imprecise, this chapter details several well-known traits of likable persons.

**There are two strategies to increase your likeability before speaking with someone.**

Before you have even spoken, people begin to build an opinion about your likeability. The first approach to appear more likable is to improve your physical attractiveness: by clothing and grooming well, staying in shape, and projecting a confident body language. Even if you are unable to transform into Adonis, every little effort helps. Individuals who appear attractive and well-dressed are perceived to have more appealing personalities. This is referred to as the halo effect. Of course, attractiveness is somewhat subjective, and you will want to tailor your actions to your social objectives and the types of people with whom you want to make a favorable impression.

An item of clothing or haircut deemed attractive in an artsy neighborhood of a large metropolis may not be deemed so elsewhere.

Additionally, your reputation and accomplishments can influence how others perceive you. Have you ever seen someone from afar and thought they were unremarkable, but then a friend mentioned something they did and that impressed you? It predisposes you to view them more positively when you speak with them. The opposite can occur if you are aware of someone's jerkiness. You cannot actively manage this point, as you may with the others who follow, but it may affect how others perceive you as you gain accomplishments.

**Possessing the ability to communicate your individuality**

You want to avoid appearing unlikable. Another possibility that is nearly as unpleasant is for people to meet you and form no impression at all. This can occur if you are excessively shy or silent or so afraid of saying the wrong thing that you discuss everything in a very safe, bland manner. You do not have to become particularly outgoing or assertive with your thoughts or jokes, but you need to demonstrate enough of your personality to elicit a response.

**Maintain a reasonable level of confidence.**

On the whole, people value other peoples' confidence. This is not to mean that you must come across as a self-assured salesman. That may be excessive. Be at ease with yourself. Certain people are likable when they are a bit shy or odd but own it rather than seem ashamed or embarrassed.

**Maintain a reasonable level of cheerfulness and optimism.**

Generally, likable individuals are happy. They see the bright side of everything. They do not complain frequently, and even when they do, they do not allow their energy to become too negative.

They can complain about their obnoxious employer while still making it sound like an enjoyable story. A joyful emotional state is pleasant to be around and has an infectious quality. Again, you are not required to be perpetually cheerful or never express a bad emotion or opinion. Strive to maintain a healthy balance of positivity and negativity.

**Appear to be a people person.**

People often find someone more likable if they appear to care about other people and them. On the other hand, people often despise somebody who comes across as arrogant or aloof. Some persons are misanthropic on the inside yet are likable on the outside due to their apparent friendliness and personability. While it is admirable if you enjoy the majority of individuals you encounter, achieving that trait is more difficult. Some of us are more selective than others regarding who we want to converse with or become friends with. You can still make an effort to maintain a cheerful demeanor in your interactions:

- Demonstrate friendly and receptive body language by smiling, maintaining nice eye contact, and giving people your undivided attention.

- Engage in communication with others.

- Chat eagerly with anyone who initiates contact with you.

- Take an interest in the opinions of others.

- If you do not have time to speak with someone, at the very least, greet them cheerfully.

- Contribute something to your interactions.

Apart from their ability to make others feel good about themselves, likable people possess traits that make them pleasurable to be around.

They are truly amusing, have interesting things to say, are enjoyable to be around, and are excellent listeners, among other qualities. Again, this is a subjective assessment. To one group, a dark or cheesy sense of humor may be humorous. One person may find a particular point of view interesting, while another may find it pretentious.

You may increase your likeability by honing your social skills. Perhaps you are quite amusing but might need to improve your sense of humor. Alternatively, if being amusing is not your thing, you may focus on discussing interesting topics instead.

**Possess a greater number of good than negative personality traits.**

In a chapter replete with generalizations, this one is even broader in scope than the others. A likable person may be lazy at work and irresponsible with money, yet they exhibit largely positive personality traits when engaging with others. They frequently have weaker socializing-related personality defects. Additionally, they are conscious of their vexing traits and may turn them into something endearing. For instance, if they are a little opinionated and volatile, they can catch themselves mid-rant and mock themselves for being such a hothead. They do not indiscriminately erupt at people with no regard for their annoyance factor.

It is impractical for this book to describe every possible positive and negative character feature or instruct you on reconstructing your personality completely. All you can do is become aware of your strengths and shortcomings and attempt to modify or eliminate any traits that may irritate others.

## 6.2 Being Fun

People who are enjoyable to be around are just fun to be around. However, enjoyment has a time and a place. When you are at a party or in a cheerful mood, you want to be around others who are having fun and being having fun yourself. If you are going for a quiet, contemplative walk with a friend, that same lighthearted behavior is generally inappropriate.

There are two components to increasing your enjoyment. Some behaviors increase your enjoyment, and there are traits to avoid that decrease your enjoyment. This chapter discusses both points through which young teens can learn how to become more friendly and have fun.

As with likability, the traits that make someone enjoyable are unique and tailored to your personality style. You can maintain a more subdued level of amusement. There is more to it than leaning against a table and holding a beer funnel. While everyone might be enjoyable in their manner, this section defines "fun" as having quirky, interesting, or humorous interactions with others. If someone were to declare, "My concept of fun is to spend an afternoon quietly contemplating my garden," what is said here would conflict with their definition of the word. If outgoing fun is not a priority for you, you can skip this section.

**Individuals can exist in a variety of social modes.**

At times, individuals desire a low-key, analytical, logical discussion about politics, parenting ideas, anxieties, and insecurities. At other times, people want to have fun, make stupid jokes, have a good time, and let off steam. Neither kind of social interaction is superior or inferior to the other. Both have their advantages and disadvantages. It is similar to how you are not always in the mood for a dark, dismal drama when you choose a film.

Certain individuals thrive in serious, rational social circumstances but struggle when confronted with a more frivolous, party-oriented one. They may feel out of place or irritated that everyone is not behaving more refined. Accept that not every circumstance must be grave and cerebral, and endeavor to embrace your own lighthearted, immature side if you believe that way.

**Several general ways to have fun**

- Set out specifically to have a good time. Avoid approaching the evening with the mindset of "Let us simply hang out and do nothing."

- Make fun of things and be entertaining. Inform your audience with amusing stories, clever insights, and engaging stunts.

- Introduce new activities and circumstances to people by introducing them to for instance, "Rather than sitting around, how about we sign up for karaoke," or "How about we check out the new stand-up comedy club."

- Assist individuals in having more enjoyment than they ordinarily do. Without being forceful, assist them in moving beyond their normal level of reserve. For instance, "Let us go speak with those people... Not to worry. They appear to be friendly. Let us proceed."

- Be a little more adventurous and impulsive than usual. Alternatively, to employ a cliché, say yes to more things than you would normally.

- Experiment a little bit more than you typically would. For instance, take your jokes to a bit more absurd level or accept your friend's silly bet when you normally would not.

- Have tiny skills and abilities that add to your enjoyment. For instance, knowing how to play darts or memorizing a few jokes or card games might help you and your companions have a good time together.

## Be less "unpleasant."

The traits that contribute to your lack of enjoyment are clearer and more straightforward than the abstract concepts listed previously. Once again, this section is focused on a particular concept of enjoyment, and these traits are not always detrimental in other situations.

- Do not be the person who is never in the mood to try something new or much of anything.

- Avoid being the person who wants to give up halfway through.

- Wherever you are, resist the urge to sit back and do nothing. Occasionally, this is unavoidable if you are timid or uninterested in what everyone is engaged in, but try to remain as integrated as possible.

- Avoid being too particular about the type of entertainment you require. Make the most of your circumstances and avoid becoming someone who can only enjoy themselves in the ideal setting with the ideal music choices, crowd, and drink prices. Never assume that where you are now, is uninteresting and that the fun must be in the next area.

- Attend to the amusement rather than waiting for it to come to you. Create your entertainment. Expect your buddies to bear no responsibility for your enjoyment. Avoid thinking, "I will have fun only if the band plays better tunes."

- Avoid being a downer by talking excessively about your activities or bringing up dismal or serious subjects during a good night out.

- Avoid being excessively frugal with your money. There is nothing wrong with being thrifty, but some activities require you to spend money to enjoy them, for example, do not visit an amusement park and then refuse to purchase ride tickets, play games, or purchase food.

Having fun is not immature or beneath you. Everyone can have a good time. This is not something that only stupid, absent-minded individuals do.

### Overcoming traits that stifle enjoyment

Being excessively self-conscious or serious and having fun are incompatible. You cannot unwind, have fun, or relax if you are angry with everything or everyone.

The following are traits of an uptight person:

- Regarding other people's actions as careless and thoughtless. For instance, everyone should always follow the regulations and maintain a morally upright demeanor.

- Being bothered by minor social annoyances that the majority of people overlook.

- Believing that you must constantly be in charge, proper, and well-behaved.

- Consider yourself a polished, sensitive, intellectual adult, and despise what you perceive to be childish, immature behavior.

Here are some suggestions about how to lighten up:

Recognize that you cannot control everything.

At the heart of some people's arrogance is a desire to exert control and have everyone behave according to their wishes.

You can achieve greater relaxation if you let go of this urge and accept that individuals will behave in ways you do not approve of or anticipate.

**Acquaint yourself with a more realistic expectation of what to expect in social circumstances.**

Numerous mildly vexing, yet common and unavoidable, behaviors and situations will arise while socializing. Friendships will be erratic. The venues will be loud and busy. Individuals will behave crudely and immaturely. Minor regulations and laws will be disregarded (for example, people will litter and play their music too loud at parties). The majority of people understand that these things are part of life and do not allow themselves to be too disturbed by them. If you are more socially inexperienced, the same things can grate on you because you have the false expectation that a scenario should unfold in a specific way and then become enraged when others "destroy" it.

**Make a conscious effort not to take oneself too seriously.**

It is acceptable to be a normal, dopey human being. Engaging in lowbrow activities such as watching dumb movies with your pals while talking and cracking lowbrow jokes is acceptable. It is acceptable to have lighthearted, brainless fun. You will not be able to reclaim your Intellectual card. Nobody will be concerned. Indeed, they will likely appreciate that they can be themselves with you without fear of being judged.

# 6.3 Assertiveness Skills

Assertive communication occurs when you look out for or advocate for your rights and wants in a confident, straightforward manner while remaining respectful of the other person. While assertiveness skills are frequently discussed in terms of intimate relationships or the workplace, they are also necessary for a wide variety of everyday social situations.

Knowing how to be aggressive provides a variety of advantages. Your self-esteem will naturally increase if you are willing and capable of standing up for yourself and refusing to be talked down or coerced into doing things you will regret later. Knowing how to be aggressive instills self-confidence and control in you. It makes life more joyful because you can meet your needs, pursue your goals, and avoid circumstances and activities that are not enjoyable. It is a quality that others admire. Finally, if you wish to live a less conventional social life, you will need to develop the ability to advocate for yourself and reject outside pressure.

**How to strengthen your assertiveness abilities?**

You may increase your assertiveness by altering your attitude and acquiring practical, effective assertive behaviors.

**Believe in the importance of your wants, rights, and worldview.**

One of the primary reasons people are not aggressive is that they believe their demands are unimportant or unworthy of being advocated for. They lack confidence in their own beliefs, opinions, and preferences and enable others to override them (for example, they dislike nightclubs but have swallowed the notion that they are strange or antisocial for feeling that way, and have allowed their friends to convince them to go). You must cultivate an attitude that your needs and worldview are legitimate and deserving of protection.

**Develop some assertiveness methods.**

By mastering some fundamental assertiveness tactics, you can deliver and adhere to your message in a calm, self-assured manner. If you encounter resistance, you can avoid being flustered and succumbing or becoming enraged and allowing your dialogue to devolve into more aggressive, confrontational territory.

**Confidently and plainly express your desires.**

Once you have collected the courage to act, assertiveness is quite simple: Convey your desires in a controlled, self-assured manner. You do not need to include a slew of justifications and explanations. For instance, if you are at a party and your friends are pressuring you to consume more alcohol than you prefer, you can respond, "Thank you, but no. I am no longer drinking." If you are out with a friend and they are more focused on their phone than on you, you can say something like, "Could you perhaps save it for when we are not having a conversation?" Again, you do not have to be excessively firm and assertive. While assertiveness may be necessary if someone is truly crossing a line, you may frequently be assertive in a friendly, casual manner.

**Employ "I" statements.**

A common piece of assertiveness advice is that when you urge someone to cease doing something that concerns you, you should word your message in such a way that the spotlight remains on you and your feelings. That is preferable to attacking the other person, which violates their rights, puts them on the defensive, and increases the likelihood of an unproductive argument erupting.

For instance, if your friend occasionally becomes a little too scathing and personal in their taunting of you, you could ask them to stop by being assertive in a certain manner like, "When you bring out my personal weaknesses to mock me, you hurt my feelings and make me feel uneasy about myself. I would like you to stop."

**Utilize the technique of the broken record.**

Much of the work of assertiveness comes from defending your position after you have given your original statement. They may argue, harass you, cast doubt on your character, become upset, pour on the guilt trips, gently hint they will quit hanging out with you if you refuse to comply, or declare you have no choice but to comply. It can be difficult to avoid the social tensions that this generates. The broken-record approach involves repeatedly repeating the same assertive statement until they give up. You are leaving them with nothing, preventing an argument from erupting. The best benefit of this strategy is that it eliminates the need for you to think under duress. All you have to do is repeat yourself.

**When it comes to boldness, stick to your guns.**

When you first begin acting more assertively, you may encounter some pushback from others. If your friends, family, partner, or coworkers have become accustomed to getting what they want from you, they may take offense if you begin advocating for yourself. They may make statements about how selfish or unpleasant you have become, or they may intensify their pressure techniques. It is not necessary that they are nasty and preferred you when you are soft and timid; it is simply that people are occasionally thrown off by change and will attempt to coerce you back into behaving the way they expect. Although the transition may be difficult, you will eventually acquire respect when you demonstrate your commitment to having more solid limits. If you lose an eccentric exploitative, or rude buddy, it is not a loss.

# Chapter 7: Developing and Growing Friendships

This is the final portion of the book, which discusses meeting friends, developing a social life, and overcoming loneliness. Even if you enjoy spending time alone, you will feel lonely if your minimal need for social contact is not met. Loneliness may wreak havoc on your happiness and self-esteem. It is discouraging to find yourself alone for the seventh Friday night in a row. The good news is that it is extremely simple to learn how to make friends, so much so that if you are unfamiliar with the process, you may notice benefits immediately after learning the techniques and practicing them. If you can manage your shyness and maintain a conversation, you should use the suggestions in this area to improve your social life.

When one source advises another on "how to make friends," they choose one of two approaches:

The first approach is to create positive personality traits that will help you become a more attractive buddy (being a good listener, being loyal, etc.).

The second approach describes the practical, actionable steps involved in meeting new individuals and building relationships. We discussed the first strategy in the previous; this section will discuss learnable, repeatable tactics. Individuals who are proficient at establishing friends frequently adhere to the concepts outlined in this section.

### The fundamentals of building friendships

The fundamental steps in developing relationships are as follows:

- Make some new acquaintances.

- Invite and schedule activities with those potential friends.

- Once you have established some acquaintances, steadily deepen the bonds.

- Repeat the preceding steps until you have created as many friends as you like, whether a small group of close friends or a large group.

Individuals who struggle with their social life frequently get in trouble with one or more of these processes. This list appears straightforward. However, each of the mentioned topics delves into greater detail.

## 7.1 Developing Friendships

Several points to consider as you attempt to develop a social life.

Remember that, as with any task you have not mastered yet, the process of making friends will be easier and more enjoyable if you approach it with the proper mindset and expectations.

**Being alone does not imply that you are fundamentally flawed.**

Lonely persons frequently view their limited social lives as a reflection of their brokenness and unlikability. Loneliness is frequently a consequence of an unhealthy lifestyle and social behaviors that inhibit meeting new people and building relationships. Everyone can experience loneliness if they do not engage in acts that foster friendship. Someone popular and socially connected in their hometown would feel isolated in a new place if all they do is commute to work and then return home to watch TV. Many people develop friendships without realizing it, and they are unsure how to intentionally form a new social circle when they move to a new place.

Being alone does not inherently imply that you have an unpleasant, off-putting demeanor. Numerous irritating persons have large social circles due to their proficiency and activity in the specific skill of making acquaintances. Numerous charming, intriguing people are more isolated than they would like to be due to their lack of proficiency in those same skills.

**Attempting to make friends does not imply that you are stupid, desperate, or in need.**

Many people desire friendship but are afraid that aggressively seeking it will imply desperation or groveling. That is not the case. There is nothing pitiful about making friends or showing interest in others. It is a daily activity that self-assured, sociable individuals engage in. Even if the occasional individual views you as desperate, you must have the mindset that it is all about you and that you will do whatever it takes to build the relationships you desire. Who cares if a few people think you are a little too enthusiastic along the way if everything works out in the end?

**Avoid self-inflicted handicaps by attempting to conceal your loneliness.**

Lonely people can become trapped in a self-defeating loop; they are ashamed of their loneliness and want to conceal it, which prevents them from engaging in activities that would enable them to meet friends. They avoid meet-ups for fear of alerting others to their desire for a more social life. They avoid inviting a classmate out for fear of disclosing that they do not have plans. As their loneliness worsens, their desire to save face grows stronger, and they are forced more into solitude. In truth, no one knows if you lack friends, and even if they do, they are probably unconcerned.

Everyone has times in their lives when they feel the need to revitalize their social circle. Whether they have relocated to a new place, grown distant from their old pals, or their earlier group gradually dwindled as members moved away or became too preoccupied with job and family.

**If you desire a social life, you must create it for yourself.**

It is critical to take the initiative as a teen as it will help you shape your life in better ways. The quality of your social life is directly related to the amount of effort you put into it. A common error made by lonely people is to wait for others to initiate friendship passively, then assume they are faulty when no one invites them out. Sometimes, but not always, people will initiate contact. If you want a group of friends, accept that you will have to exert considerable effort.

**Take it in a positive manner if others appear indifferent to you.**

This pertains to the initial point. Lonely people frequently question what they are doing wrong and why no one appears interested in spending out with them. Generally, it is not personal. Other people are frequently thoughtless, distracted, and harmlessly shackled to their routines. They would be delighted to hang out with you, but they would never think to ask you. Occasionally, you must demonstrate an interest in others and spread the word that you are open to new friendships before you emerge on their radar.

**Recognize that it may take time**

You can quickly establish a new social life in the appropriate conditions, such as when you relocate to a new city for college or join the perfect club or team and instantly bond with everyone there. At other times, your social life may take longer to come together.

It may take some time to find people with whom you are compatible, and then, if everyone is busy, it may take several months before you are all hanging out frequently. Persevere and avoid making hasty decisions.

## 7.2 Finding Potential Friends

The first step toward making friends is to identify potential candidates. That is an unsurprising place to begin, yet it is where some of the more isolated individuals become stuck. They do not expose themselves to a sufficient number of possible new friends. This chapter discusses the two primary methods for prospecting: using existing contacts and meeting new individuals.

### Make use of your existing contacts

While drawing on existing contacts will not work if you have recently relocated to a new place and do not know anyone, you will likely find the seeds of a social life nearby. You are not required to meet dozens of strangers. It is frequently easier to convert existing contacts into true friends than scavenge for new ones. You may already know a few people who may become part of your new social circle:

- People from work or school with whom you get along but have never socialized;

- Acquaintances with whom you are comfortable when you run into each other but never see otherwise;

- Friends of friends who you bonded with when you met in the past;

- Persons who expressed an interest in becoming your buddy in the past but you never accepted the offer;

- People you meet extremely infrequently but could see more frequently;

- Friends with whom you have lost contact;

- Cousins who live nearby and are your age.

**Make some new connections**

Enhancing your current relationships can be beneficial, but this is not always possible. Fortunately, there is an infinite number of locations where you can meet new people.

You will almost certainly have to coerce yourself out of your routine and prioritize meeting new people. Certain lonely persons develop a routine to spend their time at home when they are not at work or school. If this describes you and you want to meet new people, you must shake things up and venture out more. You may need to schedule some more social activities or encourage yourself to get out and do stuff in the evenings when you would typically be relaxing alone.

You may need to experiment with a few different locations for meeting people before finding one that works. Making new acquaintances is frequently one of those circumstances when 20% of your efforts yield 80% of the rewards. You may attend many meet-ups, classes, or events and find that they are all a bust, but you will almost certainly meet a slew of interesting individuals at the next one. Do not be disappointed if you join a group or two and discover that the other members lack promise. Do not generally declare that clubs "do not function" as a means of meeting new people. Experiment with different ones. Recognize that many places where you can meet people are not optimally set up to facilitate connections and that you may occasionally have to make the best of a less-than-ideal hand dealt with you. Avoid suffocating yourself by pursuing the ideal set of circumstances. For instance, you may enroll in some art programs and feel there is insufficient opportunity to meet new people because individuals come and go.

There are few opportunities to converse during the lectures. You will need to determine whether the scenario is ultimately stacked against you. You should seek alternative employment or whether a few adjustments could make it work (for example, showing up earlier to give yourself more time to chat with your classmates).

## Characteristics of good meeting places

Certain locations are more conducive to making new friends than others. The more of the following criteria a location meets, the better:

- It enables you to connect with people who share your interests, are easy to get along with, and are the types of potential friends you are searching for.

- It is a place where the scenario automatically breaks the ice for everyone and offers them reasons to speak with one another.

- It enables you to be a long-standing member or a regular and see the same people multiple times, allowing you to get to know them without feeling rushed gradually.

- It has a core of regulars, but more are constantly added.

## Approaching and becoming familiar with others

Once you are at a location with several potential buddies, you should initiate talks and attempt to get to know them. While you are unlikely to get along with everyone you interact with, if your environment contains a sufficient number of your type of people, you should get along with at least a few of them. Perhaps you will connect immediately or develop a rapport over a few weeks through smaller interactions. In either case, after you connect with someone, you can refer to them as cordial acquaintances or as context-specific "friends" (for example, work friends).

The next step is to invite them out and schedule time together.

## 7.3 Making Plans

After meeting some people with whom you click, the next step is to arrange to meet them outside of the context you met. This is a critical phase and one in which lonely individuals frequently fail. You can meet as many people as you want, and they will think highly of you, but if you do not make an effort to spend time with them, you will not build many lasting relationships. Your potential pals will remain like the colleague you speak within a class, the group you converse with during your lunch break at work, or the guy you joke around with at your rec league games. Even if you develop a strong bond with someone in that atmosphere, if you do not extend the relationship to the outside world, it may fade away when the semester ends, they obtain a new job, or the season concludes.

This chapter discusses how to create plans with others to socialize and improve your relationship. It describes how to organize your gatherings—both with individuals and groups—and how to participate in others' events. Additionally, it discusses certain critical habits and mentalities to keep in mind when formulating plans.

The concepts in this chapter are critical for establishing a new social life, but they are also extremely beneficial for maintaining or growing an existing one. When you are skilled at planning, you can truly take control of your social life and establish the type of social life you desire for yourself, rather than having to conform to whatever everyone else decides. The ability to coordinate plans is so powerful that even those with less than stellar personalities can have a busy social life simply by constantly planning one outing or another.

Meanwhile, someone who is more enjoyable or intriguing but sluggish at organizing get-togethers may not go out as much as they would like.

**Two beneficial practices**

To increase your chances of effectively making plans with others, develop the practice of doing two things.

1. **Request people's contact information shortly after meeting them.**

   You may meet someone interesting, but there is no guarantee that you will see them again shortly. Inquire about their phone number or email address, or check to see whether they are members of whatever social networking site your location and age group frequent. That way, they will be easy to contact if you choose to arrange a meeting. Additionally, if they have your information, they can contact you to chat or invite you somewhere.

2. **Maintain an up-to-date technological knowledge base.**

   Events are frequently promoted and organized through social networking sites, even in some cases exclusively via them, so join whichever ones your peers use. You do not have to appreciate or use them frequently, but you should take advantage of the social changes they facilitate.

**Understanding how quickly you can extend an invitation**

How much time should you spend getting to know someone before inviting them out? There is no correct answer. If you have struck up a quick rapport, it is OK to invite someone out immediately. It is also OK to have an initial favorable impression of them but wish to learn more about them before inviting them anywhere. However, you may not always have the choice of going slowly.

If you have met someone you are unlikely to see again, you can continue to learn more about them via messaging or social media, but for the most part, you need to act on the lead before it goes cold. In some circumstances, you may have loved your initial conversation with them but be skeptical of your compatibility if you spent more time together. Again, there is no correct course of action. You could take a chance and ask them to do something, even though the chemistry may not exist. Alternatively, you may extend an invitation just when you are quite certain you will enjoy their company.

**Try to establish recurrent plans.**

Typically, once you have spent time with a person or group, you will need to go through another round of making plans to see them again. That is hardly an insurmountable amount of labor, but it can give the impression that your social life is in flux from week to week. You may attempt to establish a recurring schedule, such as watching a movie at someone's house every Wednesday night or going out to dinner once a month. Often, everyone is too busy to maintain an ongoing arrangement, but it is wonderful to develop these dependable social activities for yourself. Maintaining these agreements requires effort, so do not take them for granted. At times, people will become sidetracked by other elements of their lives. It may take some work to gather everyone each time, so be flexible about canceling or rescheduling as necessary. Additionally, these plans function better when a larger group is involved. Even if only half of the members can attend each time, there are still enough people present for them to be enjoyable.

**Apart from making your plans, there are other ways to meet people.**

This chapter discussed how to make your plans, which is the most critical skill because you directly influence them.

However, there are other methods to socialize without doing much work yourself:

**Be invited to socialize**

While it is wonderful when others invite you to spend time with them, you should never rely on it and always be prepared to create your plans. However, when it comes to learning about other people's plans:

**Accept every invitation that comes your way.**

If you are attempting to have a social life and someone invites you to anything, make every effort to attend. Why would you pass up an opportunity to get out there? When you have more friends and invitations competing for your time, you may be more selective. If you are more anxious or solitary, it is natural to overthink an invitation and come up with reasons why it will not be enjoyable. Overcome your fears and go anyway. You never know how delightful something will be unless you go and experience it for yourself.

Occasionally, you will have to burden yourself to maintain your social life. You can be invited to a movie you are not very interested about or be invited to a party at the last minute on a cold, rainy Friday night when you intend to sleep in early. Once again, the benefits of being in a social atmosphere exceed these tiny inconveniences.

If you decline too frequently, most people will stop inviting you out. They may have no animosity toward you, but the next time they plan an event, they will think, "They have never shown up when I have asked before, so there is no use in notifying them this time." If you are interested in an invitation but are unable to attend due to valid reasons, communicate to the inviter that you would love to hang out with them if you could. The simplest approach to demonstrate this is to extend your invitation shortly afterward.

**Determine what other people's interests are and then jump on board.**

Many people continually have things to do with their friends because they inquire about everyone's whereabouts frequently. They do not attempt to launch their plan every week. If they wish to go out on the weekend, they will begin pinging their social circle on Thursday, inquiring about their plans for Friday night and the weekend. They will jump on board if they hear anything they like. If no one has concrete plans, but some people are interested in doing anything, the "asking around" chat serves as a jumping-off point for determining what they could accomplish together (for example, "We could have a barbecue at the park-like Morgan was talking about the other day"). Additionally, asking around demonstrates initiative, it demonstrates a desire to spend time with others, and keeps you on a group's radar.

## 7.4 Strengthening Your Friendships

Not every friendship has to be extremely close. Individuals are frequently content to have some friends who engage in lighter activities or are party companions. However, we normally require at least one deeper and more intimate friendship. This chapter discusses the aspects that contribute to friendships growing stronger. While the concepts discussed here frequently occur naturally when a friendship develops, you can have some control over your relationships by consciously attempting to apply them. They are primarily applicable to individual friends, although some of them also apply to collective friendships.

### Methods for establishing a lasting friendship

Each friendship is unique, and not every point will apply equally to each type. Certain friendships are more focused on sharing and connecting, while others focus on hobbies, joking around, and going out at night.

### Increase your time spent together.

Spending more time with someone is the foundation for developing a stronger friendship with them. A close bond does not develop over a few hours. You require room for all of the relationship-enhancing activities discussed below to occur. Time is a significant component in our friendships, and we frequently develop strong bonds with those with whom we have frequent contacts, such as coworkers, friends of friends, classmates, and team members. Over time, friendships can emerge between individuals who were previously indifferent to one another.

**Make an effort to see them regularly.**

The primary approach to spend enough time with someone is to see them frequently. Occasionally, you will find yourself in a circumstance where you are forced to work those times. If not, you should attempt to organize get-togethers using the preceding chapter's suggestions to continue seeing them. With some folks, you will rapidly develop a routine of constant socializing. With others, you may only be able to meet for a quick bite to eat every three weeks.

**Spend time speaking with them one-on-one.**

While it is possible to meet and engage with others in a group situation, the real opportunities to connect frequently occur when you are alone with one other person. Additionally, if you have not spent time alone with someone, how close is your friendship? Many people had met someone through group activities but saw a different side of them when they began hanging out in pairs. They will look to that as the point at which their friendship truly blossomed. You may obtain that one-on-one time by arranging for them to do something separate with you. You could also find opportunities to separate yourself from the larger group with them. For instance, the two of you might be able to go to the garden during a party to converse.

**Have a nice time when you meet.**

What constitutes a "good time" varies according to your objectives. It may be an academic discussion over coffee, an afternoon spent together working on a car, or a night out in the town. You can contribute to the growth of a friendship by making an extra effort to do activities you know your new acquaintance will love. As indicated earlier, you do not have to accomplish anything original every time. On the other side, avoid becoming stuck in a rut where all you do is sit and get bored.

**Learn more about one another and broaden the scope of your conversations.**

When you are not very close to someone, you are familiar with their basic biographical information. Your interactions frequently revolve around a few topics, such as your common workplace or a sport you both enjoy. We feel more connected to someone when we learn more about them and can discuss various topics.

**Be open to each other**

While not every friendship requires extensive intimate sharing, people perceive their relationships to be richer and more fulfilling when discussing difficult or personal matters with someone they trust. It can also be satisfying to know that you have revealed portions of your "true self" to someone, and they accept you for it, or to connect when you discover you share a common hidden quirk or prior experience. You should make a conscious effort to lead your new acquaintance's chats toward more in-depth areas if they do not naturally progress in that direction over time. If your friend initiates the more intimate direction, do not be afraid.

**Have some adventures or crazy times together.**

Having a shared past with someone reinforces the idea that you have a deep connection with them. Even better is a history peppered with truly remarkable events. It enables you to remark, "Ha-ha, remember when we..." Many people recall perceiving someone, or a group, as casual friends until they embarked on that one famous camping trip together and developed a strong bond. An adventure is an enjoyable and unusual tour or event.

**Be there for them in their moments of need.**

When one person assists another, they can form bonds. They can also become closer when they assist one another in overcoming a common obstacle, whether it is a hard-graduate program, working for an obnoxious boss, or living together as broke aspiring entrepreneurs. They can reflect on the relationship and conclude, "We are getting there. We have helped one other get through some difficult times." It is more difficult to view someone as a casual buddy after witnessing their vulnerability, having them lean on you, and empathizing with their hardships.

As is always the case, this does not ensure that you will become closer, and you may even feel used and unloved. However, if the friendship is going well, assisting one another might help it grow even stronger. Although significant life events foster stronger relationships, assisting a new friend can be as easy as offering to drive them to the mechanic to pick up their car or allowing them to vent about something thoughtless, their brother said.

# Conclusion

If you continuously apply the concepts in this book over time, your social condition will improve. You will feel reasonably secure and at ease in your surroundings. While you will not be fearless, you will be able to navigate most social situations without feeling too nervous or scared. You will be able to carry on most conversations without difficulty, and you will understand that it is not completely your responsibility if one does not go well. You will develop a social life that is conducive to your well-being.

It is critical and beneficial to read about developing social skills, establishing friendships, and forming friend groups. This, however, is only half of the struggle. To enjoy the benefits of the seeds sown in this book, you must get out there and put them into practice.

Your initial step should be to choose one or two critical areas to practice with current friends and family members. If nothing stood out, storytelling and increasing your awareness of your social shortcomings would be an excellent place to start.

Make a concerted effort to achieve mastery on these fronts. There is no reason why you cannot become one of the world's top 1% storytellers. It is merely a skill and one that only a small percentage of individuals actively practice. We all have social shortcomings, but many people have whittled them down to the point where they are barely obvious.

**Pitfalls associated with increased social awareness.**

As your social skills improve, there are no major hazards to avoid. It is almost all positive. One potential issue is that you may acquire certain undesirable habits as you venture into new social areas.

For instance, if you previously avoided taking the lead in conversations but suddenly like doing so, you may notice that you frequently interrupt others or make inappropriate jokes. You can identify and repair those errors in the same way that you did with other old habits.

## Maintaining your momentum

Once you have improved your communication and friend-making skills, the benefits are permanent. You will not forget how to manage a given scenario if you know how to do so. It is not like losing weight, where there is always the possibility of regaining the pounds if you are not attentive. If you do not use the skills for a while, they may become rusty, but this will pass quickly. In practice, conversation skills are so frequently employed in daily life that you will be able to keep them without exerting excessive effort. Your courage to put yourself in awkward social settings may deteriorate more rapidly if you do not continue to push your comfort zone. However, it is easier to regain that comfort level than it is to obtain it in the first place.

If you have always preferred solitude, your newly enhanced social life may fizzle after a while. This can occur if you lose your inner motivation to create new friends because you no longer have anything to prove to yourself. Previously, you were prodded by the agony of desiring to overcome your loneliness and social skills gaps. You may be stuck in a rut right now; you are aware that you could go out and make more friends if you so desire, but there is no rush. For the time being, you are going to stay home and watch some movies for another weekend. If you find yourself in this predicament a second time, it will be much easier to break free after you re-establish your enthusiasm to meet new people.

Additionally, your social life may level out as a result of a course correction. Once you have mastered socializing, you may experience a phase where you are constantly out and meeting new friends. You are having fun using your newly acquired abilities, compensating for lost time, and demonstrating to yourself that you can do this. However, the novelty of having "bloomed" will wear off with time, and you will revert to your genuine, more understated social inclinations.

**Handling tough situations**

Though your more refined social skills are unlikely to regress much, there are a few scenarios in which socializing may be more difficult. The first is if other elements of your life become excessively demanding or challenging. All of that additional stress and disappointment may momentarily increase your shyness and anxiety. Second, your living circumstances may change in the future, and you may find yourself in an environment where making friends is more difficult. You will be aware of the methods you will need to employ, yet the odds will remain stacked against you. For instance, you may go to a small town following graduation and struggle to make friends, as anyone would.

Allow yourself to temporarily function at a lower level if you encounter a difficult situation. It may take some time for your life to settle, and it is not a reflection of you if you feel slightly more insecure or socially uncomfortable than usual during that time. Consider what would happen if you hurt your ankle and were forced to scale back your physical activities for a few weeks—this does not mean you are permanently disabled. Utilize some more stress-reduction techniques to reduce any anxiety you may feel about socializing. Refresh any anti-anxiety or confidence-building ideas and tactics you have used in the past but have not needed to use as much recently (for example, you may need to go back to consciously questioning your counterproductive thoughts).

When you find yourself in a more practically demanding position than you are accustomed to, exercise patience and avoid putting yourself under pressure to solve it immediately. Take the time to experiment with various methods of adapting your existing skillset. Accept the possibility that you will never achieve the same outcomes as you would in more favorable circumstances. Do not hold this against yourself (for example, acknowledging there will rarely be an opportunity to meet as many potential friends as easily as you did in college).

**What should I do next?**

It is fairly uncommon for socially inexperienced individuals to believe they will not feel fulfilled and "fixed" until they achieve extreme popularity and charisma. When they achieve a functional, average level of social skills, they frequently realize that it is sufficient. Nothing prevents you from attempting to improve your people skills. As we stated earlier, being charismatic is more about performing the fundamentals slightly better than average than applying a set of specialized high-end tactics. Additionally, fundamental social skills serve as a basis for more specialized subskills. You could focus on developing skills such as flirting and dating public speaking, sales, or leadership if you have not previously.

**"How come no one has noticed how changed I am now?"**

When you set out to enhance your social skills, you may have desired validation in the form of your family or former high school friends being amazed at how much you have improved. You must accept the possibility that you will never receive such recognition. While new acquaintances will respond to the new you, those who have known you for a while will frequently perceive you as you have always been.

That is partly because if someone has a preconceived notion of what you are like, they will hunt for instances that favors their preconceived notion and disregard anything that contradicts it. Additionally, there may be a dynamic in place around certain people that prevents your adjustments from being fully apparent. While dining with your family, they will be unaware of how much more secure you are while meeting strangers at gatherings.

**Self-image**

Our self-image is frequently out of step with our current degree of achievement. Even after you have improved your social skills, you will continue to feel "awkward," "geekish," or whatever name you have given yourself for a long time. You may even feel like an imposter, fearful that everyone will suddenly come to their senses and think you are just a nerd faking it. You may find yourself including references to your former shyness in your conversations, either to preemptively explain away any blunders you may make or because you believe it is such an integral part of your personality. These feelings may never completely vanish, even though they have no visible effect on you. They may also dissipate over time, and you will begin to perceive yourself as a normal person, undefined by your previous interpersonal conflicts.

At the moment, your social troubles may appear to be an all-consuming hurricane that is wreaking havoc on your life. If you continue to work on them, they will eventually devolve into an off-handed, single-sentence account of anything from your history. You will be conversing with someone and will remark, "True. I was quite reserved in high school and college... In any case, as I was saying..."

While mastering these skills, keep in mind what is at stake. Developing stronger social skills will help you deepen current friendships and relationships with family members, create new ones, get along better with strangers and acquaintances, and instill confidence in you that you may not have had previously. Because the reward is so great, hard work is easily justified.

Once you have established that you are almost always a net contribution to the organizations you join and that your most glaring social shortcomings have been addressed, shift your attention to your social circle. Are there people with whom you spend a lot of time who are not a beneficial influence on your life? Perhaps it is time to let them make their friends. Who are the people you spend the most time with, and how can you contribute to forming a coherent friend group?

While you can begin to improve immediately, the process of socially reinventing yourself and regaining your social skills may take months, if not years. However, among those I know who have done this, the verdict is unanimous: the time spent is well worth it and maybe the best investment you can make.

CPSIA information can be obtained
at www.ICGtesting.com
Printed in the USA
BVHW031328190422
634699BV00009B/550